THE LITTLE BOOK OF
INFLUENCE

8 Keys to
Transformative
Communication

JORDANA BORENSZTAJN

THE LITTLE BOOK OF
INFLUENCE

Dedication

For everyone brave
enough to show up
fully and unapologetically

CONTENTS

Welcome — 1
Your Journey To Real Influence

Chapter One: Perceive — 10
The Secret Of Seeing What Everyone Else Misses

Chapter Two: Reimagine — 30
The Secret Of Finding Gold In Disasters

Chapter Three: Empower — 48
The Secret Of Believing In Others First

Chapter Four: Signals — 62
The Secret Language Of Non-Verbals

Chapter Five: Expression — 82
The Secret Of Language That Opens Minds

Chapter Six: Navigate 102

The Secret Of Meeting Hearts
  Before Moving Minds

Chapter Seven: Congruence 118

The Secret Of Complete Alignment

Chapter Eight: Embody 134

The Secret Power Of Being
  Unapologetically Human

**The Permission You've
Been Waiting For** 148

Let's Connect 152

About The Author 154

Endnotes 156

WELCOME

Your Journey To Real Influence

The enthusiastic chatter of 300 voices went silent. Phones disappeared, laptops were closed, and every executive in the room was suddenly laser-focused on me. In that moment, I realised I had discovered something most people spend their entire careers searching for: the secret to influence.

But rewind to 12 months earlier, when I had bombed so spectacularly on a cruise ship that passengers were wishing security would remove me while floating mid-sea. Same person. Same passion. Completely different outcome.

What changed? I learnt the difference between performing *at* people and connecting *with* them.

The Search For The Formula

What makes someone an incredible communicator? Is it their words? Tone? Timing? Or something deeper; something in the way a message is delivered so powerfully, it moves us to act?

To find the answer, my career became a relentless pursuit,

and deep exploration, of human connection. Half my life has been spent on stages in 45 different towns and cities across three continents as a speaker, MC, comedian, magician, and mentalist – and the other half spent off stage, as a journalist, public speaking trainer, and hypnotist. And each role has taught me something vital.

As a comedian, I have learnt how to read people in real time; every flicker of the eyes, every energy shift. Stand-up comedy is a live conversation and a two-way exchange in every moment. You must adapt on the fly, bounce back quickly from what doesn't land, and learn to transform failure into laughter. Presence is everything.

As a magician and mentalist, I have learnt that our brains are efficient; they default to patterns and jump to conclusions to save energy. I have spent years decoding these mental shortcuts so I can work with the mind, not against it. That moment of surprise? It's a mirror, revealing how easily we can be influenced.

As an MC, I have learnt the power of reading the room and tuning my emotional radar to become hyper-aware of what an audience needs – right now. You read subtle body language, pick up on the collective mood, sense energy shifts, and adapt instantly to create experiences where everyone wins.

As a speaker, I have learnt the difference between forgettable keynotes and ones that set a room on fire. When it's electric, people lean forward, heads nod, and there's a sparkle in their eyes. And they walk away changed; with new perspectives, renewed energy, and tools they'll actually use. That's when you know your message didn't just land – it transformed.

As a journalist, I learnt to see who was really in front of me and ask creative questions that went beyond the standard Q&A. My job was to get to the story beneath the story; making people feel so comfortable, they'd share parts of themselves they rarely revealed. When you truly see people for who they are, they give you insights you could never get from predictable questions.

As a public speaking trainer, I have learnt to see possibility in others before they can see it themselves. I help people silence their internal critic so they experience and discover a limitless version of themselves, with no constraints and no negative beliefs… just pure potential. I help them express and connect with who they really are, and watch them transform from self-conscious to connected and confident right before my eyes.

And as a hypnotist, I have learnt that deep influence begins with rapport, created before a single word is even spoken. Every pause, every tone, and every breath is deliberate. And language becomes a precision tool. Hypnosis taught me that true communication isn't about pushing an idea; it's about creating space for new possibilities to emerge.

My breakthrough came when I realised these weren't separate skills. They were all building blocks of the same core ability: the power to truly connect with another human being in real time.

So I began tracking influence obsessively, documenting every moment that worked and every spectacular failure. When I stepped back and looked at the patterns, they all pointed towards the same truth: Transformative communication always contains the same eight essential elements.

I wanted to create a mnemonic so these elements would be easy to remember. And when I outlined the key points, I saw they could be arranged to spell out the very thing that makes influence possible in the first place: **presence**.

P.R.E.S.E.N.C.E.

Perceive
Truly see and listen with your whole body.

Reimagine
Envision new possibilities and bring them to life through unwavering belief.

Empower
Believe in others so deeply that they begin to believe in themselves.

Signals
Master non-verbal cues that speak louder than words.

Expression
Use language that opens minds and creates possibilities.

Navigate
Meet people where they are, then guide them forward.

Congruence
Complete alignment between what you think, feel, say, and do.

Embody
Bring your whole, imperfect, magnificent self to every interaction.

Because when you're truly present – fully here, fully engaged, and fully connected to the moment – only then can true connection and influence take place.

Why This Matters, Right Now

We're surrounded by noise. Everyone is talking, but there's not enough true meaning being communicated. We're drowning in social media notifications, endless algorithm changes, AI-generated content that feels increasingly empty, platform updates nobody asked for, and productivity tools that unquestionably make us way less productive.

Despite popular opinion, communication isn't a "soft skill". It's the sharpest tool you've got. Your communication shapes your confidence, your career trajectory, your relationships, and your impact on the world.

This is personal for me. I've watched brilliant people stay silent in meetings because they were terrified of being judged. I've seen relationships crumble and careers stall; not from lack of talent, but from lack of connection. And I've witnessed incredible ideas wither away because their creators couldn't communicate them powerfully.

In a world of ever-increasing artificial content, authentic human connection isn't just nice to have – it's our survival skill.

The Framework That Changes Everything

Once you understand how influence really works, you'll never communicate the same way again. You'll walk into rooms differently, tell stories differently, and you'll lead, connect, and inspire with new clarity and confidence.

Because the truth is: you're already influencing every day with your words, your energy, and your intention. The magic happens when powerful words are delivered with powerful energy.

How To Use This Book

Each chapter focuses on one element of PRESENCE, built around real stories from my journey, with loads of failures that taught me more than any success ever could. They're the moments that broke me open, revealed what authentic influence really looks like, and taught me how to never be afraid again.

You'll discover how to read a room like a comedian, master the three words that unlock a person's complete potential, learn the silent language that speaks louder than words, and turn disasters into breakthrough moments.

Because influence isn't about perfection or having all the answers. It's about presence. It's about showing up fully, reading the moment accurately, and responding with complete authenticity.

What You'll Discover

This isn't just theory born from disaster. These principles have taken me from colossal public failures to sold-out Melbourne International Comedy Festival shows where I added extra performances due to demand. They've carried me from small-town community halls to conference stages across Australia, New Zealand, Japan, Indonesia, and Fiji. I've performed stand-up comedy in New York City at incredible venues like The Stand, Carolines on Broadway, Greenwich Village Comedy Club, and New York Comedy Club, as well as Flappers Comedy Club in Los Angeles.

The same framework that helped me survive public humiliation now helps thousands of people transform their communication in public speaking workshops from major cities to remote towns across Australia.

After years of studying it, teaching it, and sometimes gloriously failing at it – but also succeeding beyond what I once thought possible – I've learnt that influence is really about connection. And connection changes everything. When you can't connect authentically, you feel invisible. But when you master the art of true human connection, you don't just change your own life – you give others permission to be seen, heard, and valued as they are.

And that changes everything.

Ready? Let's begin with the foundation: Learning to truly see.

CHAPTER ONE
PERCEIVE

The Secret Of Seeing What Everyone Else Misses

"You're the worst comedian I've ever seen. Get off the ship." The heckler's voice boomed across the cruise ship show lounge. I stood frozen under the spotlight, microphone in hand, watching 200 passengers all stare at me with a mixture of disgust and confusion.

I wasn't just bombing. I was trapped at sea with this angry audience for the next three days. I hadn't just read the room wrong. I read the whole ship wrong.

The Dream Gig

At the start of my speaking career, I was transitioning from stand-up comedy and very eager to prove myself. So, when a speaking agent unexpectedly got a request for a last-minute cruise comedian, I thought it was too good to be true. Thank you, Universe!

The cruise company needed a comedian in 48 hours and, without hesitation, I said yes! I thought: floating stage, captive audience, international waters. What could go wrong?

Everything. Everything could go wrong.

The cruise company promoted me as a "Speciality Guest Act. Don't miss this!" The program listed every credential I had: Social Media Comedian. Social Media Strategist. Author. Presentation Skills Coach. At the time, I had two Melbourne International Comedy Festival shows under my belt and I was a social media comedian in the days before Instagram existed. (I was way ahead of my time.)

Because I always write custom material, I spent every moment of the crazy two-day lead-up writing cruise-specific material to open the top of my set. New jokes about endless corridors, repeating mirrors, and shoebox-sized rooms. On paper, it was hilarious. But I was missing one simple and fundamental question: Who exactly is this audience?

And So It Begins

Night one. I'm introduced as someone who takes a humorous look at how social media has changed the world. Great set-up – except that half the ship didn't know what social media was, and the other half didn't want it interrupting their bingo.

I walked on stage to polite, scattered applause and launched into my most "corporate friendly" set; social media, millennials, generational differences. The material that had audiences crying with laughter in Melbourne.

It flatlined. Silence… Blank stares… Arms crossed… One man checked his watch – twice. A woman in the front row actually turned to her husband and whispered something that made him shake his head.

Nothing landed.

I don't quite know how to describe the depth of emptiness you feel in your stomach (and soul) when a joke doesn't land. But this wasn't one joke; every single punchline was falling into a dark void.

Then came that voice from the back, a man in his 80s, and the worst heckler I have ever had: "You're the worst comedian I've ever seen. Get off the ship!"

The comedian in me wanted to heckle back with something cutting. The professional in me – the one who'd signed a contract and needed to eat – whispered: *Maybe don't get kicked off in international waters.* So, I smiled through the humiliation, finished the set, and quietly retreated.

But the night wasn't over. There were two shows. The first was brutal. The second was horrendous. Same material, fresh humiliation.

The Floating Prison Of Shame

On a cruise ship, you live with your audience. And this elderly audience really wanted me to know how much they hated my show.

During my first attempt at the buffet, a British woman looked me straight in the eye: "You're that awful comedian!"

During my second attempt, an Aussie man said: "I heard you bombed last night. That's rough. Don't sit with us, we don't want to be seen with you."

And on my third attempt, a woman loudly announced to her table, "That's her! The terrible one!"

To my surprise, one couple approached and asked to sit with me. I took a sigh of relief. For a moment, I thought I'd found allies. Instead, they requested to join me so they could give me a full download of everything wrong with my performance. The first words the man uttered were: "Your first joke offended everyone."

By the way, the joke was:

Just by a show of hands…
Who's here because you love travelling?
Who's here because you love seeing new destinations?
And who's here just to avoid your extended family members?

It's a safe opening. A classic rule of three. But, apparently, deeply unfunny.

So I gave up eating in public and my tiny cabin became my bunker. I would sneak to the cafe to buy blueberry muffins and try my best to avoid eye contact with passengers in the corridors. But I was intercepted at every corner.

One man felt compelled to explain: "I'm in my 80s, as are my friends. We don't use social media and your show didn't go well."

Another offered half a compliment: "I thought your talk was interesting, but boring." *(Umm, it wasn't a talk, buddy.)*

But my worst encounter was in the elevator, when I came face to face with the heckler again. The doors opened and I heard that booming voice: "There she is – that disastrous comedian from last night!" Complete with hardcore finger-pointing.

The entertainment director looked at me with deep concern: "I don't know why the cruise booked a social media act. It's just not right for this crowd."

We agreed: for everyone's sanity, I would not perform again. And I spent the remaining days hiding in my cabin… eating blueberry muffins.

The Flight To Redemption

Contrast this with New York when I performed one of the best sets of my entire life.

I flew into Newark, New Jersey, and the flight was complete chaos. People were yelling, screaming, and fighting. A man named Harvey was attempting to defy physics, jamming bags into overflowing overhead compartments.

And I was wedged between a couple accusing the people in front of them of having a "mysterious smell" and a guy who'd claimed half my seat as his personal territory. It was absolute pandemonium. I thought, *Where the hell am I?* It felt like I had stepped into a live taping of a US sitcom where the chaos of *Jersey Shore* met the attitude of *Everybody Loves Raymond*. Midway through this utter madness, I had one of those lightbulb moments. *This isn't travel hell. This is a full-blown comedy goldmine.*

The Breakthrough

That night, I had my first set at Carolines on Broadway – a famous comedy club just blocks from Times Square. I had polished material ready; jokes I'd perfected at the Melbourne International Comedy Festival. Safe, tried, and tested material that always got huge laughs.

But sitting there on that plane, surrounded by pure human theatre, I felt that familiar tingle of being handed material so perfectly ridiculous that my comedian brain started firing.

So I did something that terrified me: I scrapped my entire set. Right there, mid-flight.

My hands were actually shaking as I crossed out jokes I'd spent months perfecting. *Are you insane?,* the voice in my head screamed. *You're about to perform at Carolines, and you're throwing away your safety net for aeroplane observations?* But something deeper was driving me.

And so while Harvey was still causing chaos, I wrote frantically on aeroplane napkins. Fresh material about the flight, the chaos, the guy sitting over half of my seat. I trusted my gut. I read the room (well, plane) and created pure, unfiltered material about that moment.

When It All Came Together

That evening, I stood in the wings at Carolines listening to the crowd's energy – that pre-show buzz of anticipation mixed with typical New York scepticism.

I stepped on stage, grabbed the mic and began.

"So I just flew into Newark, New Jersey, and it… was… insane…"

The crowd starts laughing.

"It felt like I was trapped in the middle of an episode of *Jersey Shore*. People were yelling 'Harvey, Harvey, shove it in!'"

And as I acted out Harvey trying to cram his bag in the overhead with my best Long Island accent, the room erupted.

These were New Yorkers. Travellers. People who'd lived this exact nightmare. I could see recognition flickering across faces because these people had lived this chaos. They didn't just get the jokes; they felt them. When I got to the Harvey bit, mimicking the bag-shoving madness, a woman in the front row snorted because she was laughing so hard.

It wasn't polite laughter in that club. These were real, deep-in-the-belly laughs. And this set killed (which means it was an absolute hit, in comedy language). It was magic, and not because it was polished – far from it. But because I was present – to my experience, to the room, to the energy, and to the people right in front of me.

The Read-The-Room Lesson

The difference between my cruise ship catastrophe and this New York triumph had nothing to do with my skill level or the quality of my material. It was about *seeing* versus performing blind.

On the cruise, I was performing *at* my audience; delivering my agenda regardless of their response. In New York, I noticed the energy, the mood, and the shared experience. I adapted to what was actually happening instead of bulldozing through with what I'd planned. And I performed *with* them, creating something together in real time.

I discovered the best stand-up comedy doesn't come from perfect preparation. It comes from perfect presence.

Looking back, I can see exactly what I missed on that ship and what I finally caught at Carolines. The signals were always there, I just hadn't learnt to interpret them.

The Body Language I Missed

On the cruise, arms were crossed and bodies turned away, with feet pointed towards exits. The woman in the front row was literally angling herself away from me mid-joke; a human shield against my humour.

At Carolines, people were leaning forward with relaxed shoulders, big smiles, and with eyes locked on me instead of checking their phones. This was the universal body language of "We're with you".

The Eyes That Told The Truth

On the cruise, I saw glazed expressions and sideways glances that clearly said, "How much longer is this going to last?"

At Carolines, eyes lit up with recognition; that spark that happens when someone sees their own experience reflected back at them and thinks, "Yes, exactly!"

The Energy I Finally Felt

The cruise had dead air; the kind of silence that sucks oxygen out of a room and makes everything feel like you're pushing a boulder uphill.

Carolines was electric; the room buzzing with shared recognition. The energy built on itself, each laugh making the next one louder and richer.

The Missing Piece

That cruise taught me something massive that no standing ovation ever could: you can't avoid the full emotional spectrum of creative life. The fear. The judgement. The disapproval. You must live it, fully. And if you don't allow it to break you, it builds something else entirely: resilience, clarity, and an unshakeable belief in your work.

Stand-up comedy – like all real communication – comes in waves. Amazing one night, unbelievably challenging the next. Same material, different result; all based on who's in the room, the energy, and whether you're truly connected to the people in front of you.

Most importantly, I learnt that when you've survived being heckled at sea, booed at the buffet, told to "get off in Sydney" by someone's grandfather, and you've still managed to keep your mascara intact, nothing else in your career feels quite as scary. That's the gift.

They say the best comedy comes from truth and pain. On that cruise ship, it was truth, pain, and blueberry muffins. This experience taught me that all my comedy training meant nothing if I couldn't read the most basic signals: mood, energy, and expectations.

I had to learn to see before I could influence. And when you see differently, you communicate differently. That's when you stop performing and start connecting.

Beyond The Stage

This lesson extends far beyond floating comedy stages. Whether you're in a boardroom, at a dinner party, or giving a presentation, the same principle applies: power lies in perception.

So much of our communication lives in the unspoken. In the way a body turns. The pause before a question. The weight of a sigh. Whether someone's feet are pointed towards you, or towards the exit. Every element matters. Every element speaks.

Ever heard of the 7-38-55 Rule?[1] Professor Emeritus of Psychology Albert Mehrabian's research revealed that when delivering messages with feelings and emotion, 55% of the meaning comes from body language, 38% comes from our tone of voice, and only 7% comes from the spoken word.

Since we spend most of our energy focusing on *what* we say instead of *how* we say it, we easily miss the elements that create true connection. We're looking but not seeing. We're hearing but not really listening. We're physically present but stuck in our heads, unaware of what's happening right in front of us.

We race through our agenda, just like I did on that cruise ship, instead of reading the moment and meeting it where it is.

The Comedy Classroom

Stand-up comedy became my crash course in perception because the stakes are so high. When you're on stage with a spotlight in your face and a microphone in your hand, you've got two choices: observe everything… or experience a slow, awkward death in front of strangers.

Comedy teaches you the biggest lessons because it's uniquely brutal in how audiences respond. It's the only form of live entertainment where audiences feel entitled to interrupt and tell you exactly why you suck – while you're still performing.

In no other art form, nor in any other show that people *pay* for, is it considered even remotely acceptable to interrupt a performance. You'd never see someone stand up mid-symphony to yell, "This violin solo is trash!" And nobody interrupts *Hamilton*, *Chicago*, or *Wicked* to critique the singing and dancing.

But comedy? It's a total free-for-all. Heckle away. Walk out dramatically. Deliver your review mid-punchline. It's all fair game. And that pressure – that unpredictable, chaotic, soul-shaking pressure – is what makes stand-up comedy so incredibly challenging. But it's also what makes it the greatest masterclass in communication.

This brutal feedback forces comedians to be razor-sharp observers. We have to be. We track the tiniest shifts; empty chairs, front-row faces, smirks, fidgets, folded arms, a sideways glance, a yawn. Miss these signals and you're toast.

When dead silence stares back at you instead of laughs, you learn how to read a room instantly and pivot in real time. With three more minutes to fill, you must find a new angle, a different approach, and a way to connect that actually works.

And when you finally land *that* joke and the room erupts, that's when you understand what true connection feels like. It's not polite applause and it's not obligatory laughter. It's that magical moment when an entire room of strangers suddenly sees the world through your eyes, and the depth of connection is palpable. That's influence in its purest form.

Comedy doesn't just teach you how to influence. It teaches you how to influence while under fire.

Because if you can win over a hostile crowd with nothing but your truth and your timing… if you can turn a room of sceptics into believers using only your vulnerability and your voice… if you can recover from public humiliation and still find the courage to keep sharing your story… then you can handle any difficult conversation, any resistant audience, and any moment when your presence becomes your power.

Sharpening Your Perception

After the cruise ship humiliation, I became determined to develop the ability to read rooms, people, and moments in real time like an absolute wizard. Now, when I enter a room for an event, these are the four key elements I look for instantly, and you should too:

1. **Body Language and Positioning**
   On the cruise, arms were crossed and bodies turned away, with feet pointed towards exits. Remember the woman in the front row who was literally angling herself away from me mid-joke? A human shield against my humour? Now I know the giveaways: Are they leaning in or pulling back? Are their feet pointed towards me, or towards the nearest exit?

2. **Eyes, Face, and Expressions**

    I should have noticed the glazed expressions and sideways glances between couples that clearly said, "How long is this going to last?" Remember that man who checked his watch twice during a single joke? These tiny moments reveal what words often hide. Are their eyes lit up, or glazing over? Are they with you, or just politely staring in your general direction? Smiling with their eyes or just their mouths? Our body speaks the truth, even when our words don't. The slight frown that says *you've lost me* is critical to observe.

3. **Energy and Rhythm**

    The cruise had that dead air I mentioned before: the kind of silence that sucks oxygen out of a room and makes everything feel like you're Sisyphus, pushing his accursed boulder uphill. I learnt to feel the difference between engaged quiet and hostile quiet. Did the room go silent, or suddenly start buzzing? Did the mood shift mid-sentence? Does excitement rise or drop when you mention certain topics? Energy is invisible, but it's everything. Learn to track its rise and fall.

4. **Silence and Pauses**
   The pause before a question… The heaviness of a sigh… The moment of hesitation before someone speaks. On the cruise, those pauses were filled with judgement and disconnection. Now, I can tell the difference between thoughtful silence and uncomfortable silence. Silence is never empty. It's full of information.

Try this: Pick one conversation today and really notice. Notice not just their words, but their body language, energy shifts, and the pauses before they respond. You'll be shocked at how much information is flowing beneath the surface.

The Shift

When you develop heightened perception, everything changes. You stop talking *at* people and start communicating *with* them. You feel when conversations shift. You know when to pause, when to change course, when to dig deeper. You become the person others want to talk to because they feel truly seen and heard.

Most importantly, you learn what I learnt at sea: influence isn't about sticking to your script. It's about seeing the moment and meeting it. Perception is your superpower and the gateway to authentic influence. It's what separates the unforgettable from the forgettable.

So start noticing, start feeling, and start listening with your entire being. Because when you observe differently, you see differently, and you communicate differently. And that changes everything.

5 TRUTH BOMBS

Your perception is your superpower
Reading what's *actually* happening in a room separates the unforgettable communicators from the forgettable.

Bodies don't lie; words do
Facial expressions, postural shifts, body language, and energy reveal truth before anyone opens their mouths.

Comedy demands razor-sharp observation
Miss the signals on stage and you die publicly. Read them right and you own the room.

Presence beats polish
People trust someone fully engaged in the moment over someone perfectly scripted.

Attention is influence
When you truly *see* people, they don't just notice; they feel it instantly, lean in, and connect.

5 QUICK WINS
(TO DO RIGHT NOW)

The phone-down challenge
Ditch your phone during one full conversation. Notice how much more you *actually* notice.

The people-watching practice
Spend five minutes a day people-watching in public spaces – predicting people's next moves using only body language. Then check your accuracy.

The three-second power pause
Force yourself to count to three before responding in conversations today. The insights hiding in those pauses will surprise you.

Scan the room
Walk into your next meeting and immediately read the energy. High? Low? Tense? Then track what shifts it, and why.

Silence your internal monologue
Catch yourself mentally rehearsing your response while someone's talking. Now shut it down completely and notice what you suddenly hear.

CHAPTER TWO
REIMAGINE

The Secret Of Finding Gold In Disasters

Years before that cruise ship disaster taught me to read rooms with uber precision, I learnt something even more fundamental: how to transform the worst moments of my life into something profound and powerful.

In 2011, I went on a date that changed my life… just not in the way I had originally hoped.

I met this gorgeous guy online, and it began with such promise. He was smart, funny, good-looking… all of the things that made me mentally plan at least a few future brunch conversations together.

We had been messaging back and forth, building flirty momentum, and then it was date day.

I arrived at the café, scanning the outdoor area with nervous excitement, and then someone waved at me, and everything went downhill, fast.

I barely recognised him. He looked nothing like his picture, which had obviously been taken a decade ago – or maybe even two hairlines ago. He was hungover. Slurring. And we didn't just fail to connect but we ended up arguing. On a first date. In public. I was mortified… and I left feeling devastated.

I was in my late 20s. All my friends were in serious relationships or getting married. And here I was, walking home solo, heartbroken, and 99% convinced I was destined to become a lonely cat lady who talks to succulents.

The Call That Changed Everything

So I called a friend. But I was so shaken by the whole experience, I couldn't form actual words to explain it. All I could do was imitate him – the slurred words, the tragic timing, the whole hungover train wreck of it. By the end of the call, she was laughing. Really hard. And something unexpected happened: I felt better.

So I called another friend. This time I cranked up the drama: more exaggeration, more theatrical flair. She was laughing even harder than the first friend, and so was I. And before I knew it, we were both in hysterics and tears – that breathless laughter that makes every part of your stomach hurt.

And that laughter changed everything. It turned the whole situation around, making me forget how shocked and upset I'd felt just hours earlier. And in that moment, I discovered something I'll never forget:

Comedy is way faster – and way cheaper – than therapy. And it's the quickest way to heal.

It was a life-changing revelation.

The Mission

Right there, still reeling from the worst date of my life, I made a decision that felt both completely insane and absolutely right: I was going to become a comedian.

And I dived in head-first. I started reading comedy books, listening to audiobooks, I hired a comedy coach, I jumped into open-mic nights, and I enrolled in multiple stand-up comedy courses.

It was therapeutic, healing, creative, and so much fun. When I discovered that laughter could transform pain into power quickly, something huge shifted. I started writing jokes about everything that annoyed me. Every single frustration, inconvenience, and awkward encounter turned into a punchline. And guess what? Comedy really did become my therapy.

The more life annoyed me, the more jokes I wrote.

And before long, I had more material than stage time. Two months later, I performed my first five-minute stand-up spot at a Melbourne club. And within 18 months, I debuted a solo 55-minute show in the Melbourne International Comedy Festival.

Once I realised every bad moment could be flipped into comedy gold, my whole world changed. Bad date? Boom, new material! Unexpected argument? Brilliant content! These days, the moment I think, *Ugh, this is a disaster,* a small part of me whispers, *Ding, ding, ding – more amazing comedy material!*

No matter how bad a situation is, I know it can always be turned into epic comedy content. Having that mental cushion to fall back on turns even the worst days into some of the funniest.

Finding My Path

Learning to see life's chaos as material didn't just change how I handled bad dates – it revolutionised how I viewed every challenge, setback, and opportunity. But the path from comedian to… whatever I was becoming… was anything but smooth.

When I left the media industry, I didn't know which steps I was going to take. I had always followed my heart and passion, and I knew I wanted to do more of what made me happy.

The thing that scared me most about leaving traditional career paths was losing the income, safety, and security. But I also knew that security was blocking my ability to be as free and creative as I wanted.

I had a clear vision to become a comedian and corporate speaker, and I wanted to write my first business marketing book. I had no road map, but the destination was crystal clear.

But it got messy fast. I started social media consulting with no clients. I took a copywriting job writing about insurance policies. It was so boring and so incredibly dull. But I had the bigger picture in mind: I needed that income to fund my first book.

Was it sexy? No. Was it fun? No. Did I need to do it? Absolutely. Because I envisioned my goal, and that vision got me through writing the most mind-numbing content imaginable.

Doubting Every Step

Did I question my path? A thousand times. I questioned it

after multiple unsuccessful consulting pitches to dentists. I questioned it while writing about insurance conditions, exclusions and claims, thinking, *How did I get here?* I questioned it during slower periods when momentum felt elusive.

But I learnt to see much more than what was directly in front of me. When things didn't work out, there were greater lessons. If I was writing boring content, the joy I felt when writing my book at night was amplified a hundredfold. All those rejections from dentists meant my next proposals would be sharper. Every failure was training.

An Expansive Vision For The Future

The most influential people – the boldest leaders, the most brilliant communicators, and the people who shift culture and spark revolutions – all share one thing. They hold a vision that's bigger than the life they're living. They see what others can't yet see. They imagine what hasn't been done. And they create before anyone else believes it's possible.

I've reimagined what a comedian can bring to the corporate stage. I've reimagined what a magician can offer in the boardroom. I've reimagined what an MC can do when you blend comedy, magic, and high energy into a single, seamless thread.

I've even reimagined what a keynote speaker can be – infusing storytelling, mentalism, and moments of wonder into traditional leadership presentations.

And somewhere along the way, I realised I've been reimagining everything. Merging my worlds – journalism, stand-up comedy, photography, writing, live performance, dynamic education – into something layered, powerful, and deeply personal. What started as separate skills became parts of the same story – each one feeding the next, like a vibrant, messy, magical ecosystem I never could have predicted.

Through this totally unpredictable, deeply rewarding and incredibly fun journey, I discovered that reimagining isn't just about changing what you do. It's about becoming who you're meant to be.

The Pattern I Had Incidentally Mastered

I discovered that the same reframing skill that turned my terrible date into comedy gold also worked for everything else. I had unknowingly mastered the art of reimagining. What others saw as disconnected or scattered interests, I learnt to see as integrated strengths. What felt like professional confusion became creative fusion. What looked like risky career moves were actually strategic positioning in a market nobody else was serving.

The pattern was always there:

1. Take what seems broken, flawed, or disconnected
2. Find the hidden potential or unexpected combination
3. Embody it fully, even when others don't understand it yet
4. Trust and believe in your vision until the world catches up

This is what visionaries do. They don't just dream differently; they embody their vision so completely that the rest of us start seeing it too.

Start With Pure Imagination

We must begin by dedicating time to imagining. Not casual daydreaming and not wishful thinking, but truly imagining.

We need to believe in something so vividly that it feels inevitable. We need to open our eyes to new possibilities, step into the unknown with genuine excitement, and carry a fire that fuels the limitless potential of what could be.

When "What If?" Becomes Reality

I've had so many moments in my life where I thought: "What if?"

Not *what if* as in "Wouldn't it be nice if…" But *what if* as in: "What if this could actually happen?"

Like when I decided I wanted to meet Mark Zuckerberg. So, I dressed up as a giant Facebook Like button. *Yes, you read that correctly.* I literally made a giant costume from neoprene – the same material that surfing wetsuits are made from – and I flew from Melbourne to Silicon Valley with the goal of performing my favourite five minutes of Facebook jokes to Mark himself.

Did I meet him? (Not exactly. More on that in Chapter 4). But did I travel to Facebook's headquarters in a never-before-seen giant Like costume, pose next to the iconic Like sign, and make it onto their intranet? Absolutely.

That ridiculous adventure taught me something profound: once you have a wild dream and actually make it happen, it gives you an insane upgrade. An internal, and eternal, confidence boost, because you gain experience which builds both belief and proof. And that's when you hear your inner voice say: *Cool. What's next? Let's dream even bigger now.*

Visionaries Don't Just Dream – They Embody

What makes visionary leaders truly transformational is not that they dream differently, it's that they embody their vision so completely, the rest of us start to see it too. They become the vision so clearly and so fully that everyone around them believes it also.

Think about it. Every disruptor, innovator, icon, and magic-maker throughout history didn't just break rules. They reimagined what was possible and lived as if it were already real.

Take David Blaine, arguably one of the most influential magicians of modern times. He revolutionised magic by making one radical choice: he left the theatre. While other magicians performed behind velvet curtains for paying audiences, Blaine took magic to the streets – raw, unscripted, real. He captured something no stage magician had in this way: the pure, unfiltered shock on strangers' faces.

Or Sara Blakely, creator of Spanx. She didn't have fashion experience, but she identified a huge problem: visible panty lines and unflattering hosiery. So, she cut the feet off her own pantyhose. Manufacturers thought it was a waste of time, and her friends thought she was crazy, but she pitched relentlessly, demonstrating her idea in store bathrooms. Eventually, Neiman Marcus placed an order, Saks Fifth Avenue followed, and Oprah called[2]. Today, Spanx is worth a fortune. Blakely didn't just dream of change. She became it.

And of course, while everyone was getting around in taxis, Uber founders Travis Kalanick and Garrett Camp imagined summoning rides at the tap of a button. Reed Hastings bet on streaming at Netflix when DVDs dominated the industry, and Steve Jobs didn't just redesign phones – he reimagined them as our entire digital world. Each leader held their vision so clearly that the rest of the world eventually caught up.

That's the power of visionary influence. When someone believes so fully in a possibility, we start to believe it too – even if we don't understand it yet.

How Your Brain Creates Reality

The science behind this is powerful: when we imagine something vividly, our brains activate the same neural pathways as if we were actually experiencing it. A 2004 study out of Cleveland in the US demonstrated this beautifully: participants who imagined elbow flexion, without any physical movement, increased their muscle strength by 13.5% over 12 weeks.[3] Mental rehearsal of muscle contractions strengthened the brain-to-muscle signals, increasing actual muscle strength.

This is why visionary leaders don't just dream differently. They embody their vision so completely that their brains treat it as reality. They become it. They think the thoughts, feel the emotions, and take actions as if their reimagined reality is already here.

In hypnosis, we call this the "act as if" principle. When you behave as though your desired outcome is already true, you naturally align your thoughts, emotions, behaviours, and actions with that ideal version of yourself.

That's exactly what I was doing without realising it. While writing insurance content, I was acting as if I were already a successful author. While facing potential heckling, I was acting as if I could turn any challenge into connection. While combining seemingly unrelated skills, I was acting as if this integration was exactly what the market needed.

I wasn't waiting for permission or proof. I was becoming the vision.

How To Reimagine Your Reality

So what does this mean for us? It means that to be a truly transformational communicator – whether it's in business, on stage, or in life – we need to embody our vision, for ourselves and those around us.

The secret isn't just dreaming bigger. It's dreaming differently.

You can reimagine the big things like your career and your legacy, or you can reimagine the smaller things, too, like your morning routine and your ideal workspace.

When we imagine vividly, we expand, our vision expands, and our confidence expands because we're connected to new possibilities.

Your Reimagining Toolkit

So how do you move from imagination to transformation? Where do you begin when you want to see and feel more possibilities?

1. Feel it *before* it's real. Don't just think about your vision – experience it. Imagine you're three months or six months down the track: What does it feel like when it's happened? How are you walking? What are you saying to yourself? What are you seeing? What are you hearing?

2. Find the reframe. Every situation, no matter how awful, contains the seeds of something powerful: a truth, a lesson, some epic insight. Ask yourself: "What's the big lesson here?" A great way to uncover this is to imagine going back to yourself before it happened. What advice would you give yourself that holds the secret to your breakthrough? Or ask: 'How might this be exactly what I needed?' We don't dismiss real pain. We dig deeper to find its hidden gems.

3. Take one small, brave step. It doesn't have to be perfect. It just has to be movement towards what's calling you. Confidence doesn't come before action – it comes from the doing, even when you're afraid or unsure – and especially when it's messy! Confidence comes from taking imperfect and untested steps towards your dream.

4. Trust your inner compass over outside noise. That voice that says, *This could be something* – that's your guide. Trust your intuition and follow it, even when others can't see where you're going.

5. Document your journey. Keep a record of small wins, 'aha moments', unexpected insights, and times when your vision became real. This highlights powerful proof that progress is happening, even if it doesn't feel huge or dramatic. It also helps you identify patterns in your own reimagining process that will help you next time.

6. Share your dream with people who support you. Share your goals with people who believe in your vision and will reflect it back to you when doubt creeps in. These aren't just cheerleaders. They're anchors who will remind you of your own conviction during any tests, challenges, or shaky moments that arise.

7. Practice the "act as if" principle. Start making decisions and taking actions as if your reimagined reality is already true. How would **future you** handle this situation? What choices would they make? This embodiment is not only fun, but accelerates the transformation!

The Ripple Effect

This is how we influence from the inside out – not through pressure or performance – but through embodiment. When we truly live our reimagined reality, others start seeing it too.

People don't follow our logic. They follow our conviction and belief. And they don't invest in only our ideas. They invest in our certainty and passion about those ideas.

When you learn to reimagine one area of your life, it ripples out everywhere. My comedy mindset didn't just change how I handled bad dates; it revolutionised my entire approach to all challenges, setbacks, and opportunities.

I started seeing my diverse background not as scattered interests but as a unique combination that could create something the world hadn't seen before. Comedy plus magic plus corporate speaking plus storytelling… What if these weren't separate careers competing for time, but ingredients in a new and dynamic form of influence?

Rest assured the same pattern works whether you're reimagining your breakfast smoothie or your entire life's purpose. When you shift your perspective on one thing, you develop the muscle to shift your perspective on everything.

That terrible date and my subsequent dive into stand-up comedy taught me something profound: the most powerful leadership starts with a belief in something the world can't see yet. And, sometimes, our greatest disasters become our greatest teachers, revealing possibilities and ideas we never would have imagined without them.

So whether you're leading a team, pitching a vision, standing in front of a crowd, or mapping out a new direction for your life – start by seeing what others miss. Use those perception skills to spot the gaps, the needs, and the opportunities hiding in plain sight. Then reimagine what could fill them, using your unique set of skills. Experience your vision in your mind and body before it exists in the world and take imperfect action towards what calls to you.

As the popular ancient wisdom quote goes, "Be the change that you wish to see in the world". To that, I add… and then hold it so vividly in your mind and body that others start seeing it too.

When you combine sharp observation with bold reimagining, you don't just paint a more exciting picture of the future. You map out an entirely new path to get there. And, sometimes, all it takes is one terrible date to show you the way.

5 TRUTH BOMBS

Visionaries embody before they achieve
Great leaders don't just dream differently – they *become* the vision so completely that everyone else starts believing it too.

Your imagination is potent
Vivid mental rehearsal fires the same neural pathways as actual experience.

Feel it, then build it
Don't just visualise success, *experience* it viscerally. Feel the confidence radiating through your body, hear the certainty in your voice, and carry the energy of someone who's already won.

Action creates confidence, not the other way around
Take small, messy, and imperfect steps toward impossible goals. Confidence doesn't come from waiting. It comes from *doing*.

Reimagining isn't optional anymore
In a world that's changing faster than ever, the people who can envision new possibilities don't just survive – they dominate.

5 QUICK WINS
(TO DO RIGHT NOW)

Feel your future
Close your eyes and spend five minutes experiencing your vision as if you've already won. Feel the feelings. Hear the sounds. See the people. Smell the smells. Feel the confidence flooding your body.

The doubt destroyer
Write down your top three fears about your vision. Then cross them out and ask, "What's my next move?"

Create a victory walk
Walk for two minutes like you've already achieved your biggest goal. Put "act as if" into physical practice and feel this unstoppable energy.

Your "becoming" move
Pick one action your future self takes daily, and start doing it today. Not tomorrow... today!

Defend your dream
Next time someone doubts your vision, hold it steady and use their scepticism as rocket fuel.

CHAPTER THREE
EMPOWER
The Secret Of Believing In Others First

After learning to truly see my audience, and discovering how to transform disasters into opportunities, I thought I understood the fundamentals of influence. But there was another lesson waiting – one that would add a crucial piece to my tapestry of skills.

I had landed a very competitive cadetship at a popular tabloid newspaper at the start of my career, I worked massive hours, and I was a textbook overachiever. But I overcompensated by going overboard with time and energy because I was constantly seeking external validation.

Every story I wrote at the newspaper was inspected and checked multiple times by sub-editors. This was essential to ensure every piece was fact-checked, proofread, and seamless by the time it hit the print run. So, I was accustomed to asking and checking. Asking and checking. And ultimately, never trusting my own work.

As a result, I always assumed my work could be improved. I was terrified of spelling mistakes and of missing something crucial, and I read over everything hundreds of times before it was submitted.

I judged the value of my own work entirely based on others' reactions. The feedback was always positive, so that cycle fed itself, but I was trapped in it. I couldn't be fully proud, complete, or confident until someone else told me my work was great.

Perfectionism was my disguise for fear. What looked like ambition was, in truth, masked insecurity. My exceptional standards were driven by a desperate need for external validation. *Do they like my work? Is it good enough? Is my dress OK?* Endless questions looped around my anxious mind.

My passion was always strong – I believed I was capable of anything – but I never felt fulfilled until I got someone else's stamp of approval for something I created.

The same pattern plagued my comedy in the early years. That's why I had such extreme highs and such devastating lows. So much relied on the audience reassuring me that they liked my jokes, that they thought I was funny, and that they were confident they had made the right decision in coming to my show.

From journalism to comedy, I looked outside for validation constantly because I was missing something deep inside; an inherent sense of self-belief and confidence.

At that point, I had never worked in a setting with real autonomy. All I knew was: do your work, get it checked, then get it approved. That system fed my deep need for validation.

I was afraid to show people who I truly was. I had countless creative ideas, but I was so concerned with others' opinions that I only showed them the ambitious, driven, journalist – nowhere near the full spectrum of my true creativity.

"I Trust You"

Then came the moment that shifted everything. I remember it exactly. I was in a dream job working as National Online Music Editor at an incredible commercial radio station. I was sitting at my desk, had finally caught my boss's attention, and asked yet another question about a piece of content I was working on.

He looked at me and said, "J-Bo, **I trust you**". (He created that nickname by the way. To this day, it is still the greatest.)

That was it. No micromanaging. No constant check-ins. Just trust.

My reaction was immediate: surprise, happiness, disbelief… and complete relief. I turned around, stunned, managed a "Thank you", and felt a wave of empowerment I'd never experienced before.

It felt like freedom, like possibility. Those three words contained everything he didn't say: *Don't ask me. Just do what you do because you're brilliant.*

When someone validates you like that – in a way you've never experienced before – it's transformative. The onus was suddenly on me. The responsibility was mine. There was unwavering support and a deep level of faith that said I didn't need permission anymore. And so I gave myself permission to trust my own opinion.

The Creative Explosion

From that moment, everything shifted.

Those three words sent a powerful ripple through my body. I sat up immediately in a position of power. My chest opened. I held my head high. My physiology responded instantly to those words.

The first thing I did was turn back to the piece of content I was writing, finish it, and post it – without asking any more questions.

And everything changed after that. My confidence reached another level entirely. I stopped asking people around me if things were right or wrong. I got more creative and more free in my approach to content creation and ideas generation. I became way more expansive with my concepts. I still asked my boss for guidance when I genuinely needed it, but otherwise, everything elevated.

And during that process of working with this new autonomy, magic started to happen.

When US singer Adam Lambert visited our radio station fresh off *American Idol,* he complimented my sparkly leggings during our interview. As a diehard fan, I knew he was returning the next morning for another interview, so I did what any reasonable (aka obsessed) person would do – I raced out and bought him a matching pair.

We captured the moment I surprised him with the gift, and he loved them so much he wore them soon after, at a concert in Japan. Tight leggings, close-up photos… His fans went wild. And when they discovered we had caught the gift-giving exchange, web traffic flooded in like crazy.

None of this was planned. None of it was PR strategy. It was a spontaneous moment born from creative freedom, genuine passion, and the confidence to just act. It's the kind of authentic experience that only happens when someone trusts you enough to let you fly.

The Pattern Reveals Itself

I had worked across multiple jobs before this radio station, and not once had anyone said, "This is why you're here. Now go and do what only you can do".

But that one moment – and those three simple words **I trust you** – lit me up like nothing had before. I worked harder and smarter, with even more passion, energy, and joy. That's when I learnt something that changed how I lead: We need to believe in others *before* they believe in themselves.

Now, one of the biggest themes woven through everything I do – whether it's mentalism, comedy, MC-ing, speaking, or training others to step up and own the microphone – is this: **Believe in the version of someone they can't yet see.** The version they want to be. The version they're capable of becoming. The version buried beneath the noise of doubt, fear, imposter syndrome, and that one Grade 3 teacher who said they were either "too much" or "not enough".

Now, I believe in that new version of them before they do. And I stand beside them until they can feel and experience it too.

Belief Changes Everything

Fear is sneaky. It feels so real, so personal, and so intense. And because it's so overpowering, our fear convinces us that we're the only one experiencing it. And when that voice of fear gets loud enough, it can paralyse us, stopping us from doing the very things we know would light us up, help us grow, and fill our hearts.

But here's the magic: When someone believes in us – wholeheartedly believes in us – everything changes. It doesn't have to be a grand gesture. It can be as simple as:

"You're the best person for this role."

"What an amazing idea."

"Of course you can do this."

And sometimes, it's me saying: "You will be amazing. You can pitch. You can present. And yes, you can move your body in ways you never thought possible. And, bonus, you'll be surprised at how amazing it feels to express in this new way."

There's research that shows when others believe in us, we often rise to meet those expectations. In a well-known study from the 1960s, elementary school teachers were told certain students would show intellectual growth.

Though these students were chosen at random, they indeed demonstrated improved performance, believed to be driven by their teachers' higher expectations.[4]

What we believe about others, and how we communicate this, is incredibly powerful.

From Needing Belief To Giving It

For most of my journey, I needed belief from others. But comedy taught me how to believe in myself – even when a whole cruise ship hated me. That became one of the most crucial, foundational elements in my career and my self-worth.

Now I *give* empowerment. That's one of my main goals: to bring joy, open people's hearts, and empower them to believe in themselves – and in a version of themselves that hasn't yet emerged but is waiting to be discovered.

And so I guide them there, because once you experience that level of empowerment, where you have complete autonomy, it changes you. My boss's words sparked a breakthrough. As a result, my vision got bigger, my ideas got bigger, and my excitement exploded.

Because of these experiences, I can quickly spot others who are limited in the very way I once was. I recognise it because I've been there a thousand times, in a million different ways. But now I have learnt what lies on the other side of those limitations.

How I See What Others Miss

This insight allows me to spot the real stories behind people's resistance. When someone says "I can't" or "I could never do that" in coaching or in workshops, I don't take it at face value. I sense what the true block is – whether it's fear, anxiety, or past experiences – layered beneath what they're saying. In that moment, I help them reimagine a new version of themselves.

I get them out of their analytical mind and into their creative mind: "Let's play a game for a minute. Just imagine you're someone else; someone who doesn't have any of the fears you currently have. In fact, you love this – because you're not you." We make up a character, a role, and a new name. "Now try this exercise. What could possibly happen?"

Being playful and approaching fear in a fun way, takes the heat and pressure off, shuts down their overthinking brain, and opens up possibilities. Then we play… which is the most powerful way to learn.

Your Quirks Are Your Assets

Comedy taught me that our perceived flaws are actually our greatest assets. It was so liberating to take everything that frightened me, and everything I thought was wrong with me, and turn it all into comedy gold.

Most of us default to seeing the things that separate us as negatives. But I view every single person's differences, skills, and experiences as unique strengths. We should be proud of every distinguishing quirk and eccentricity. I know this to be completely true because I have been using my own differences as my greatest creative advantages for decades.

This lens allows me to empower people in a refreshing way. No matter what makes you different, it's a key factor that sets you apart and a unique point of difference you can use to stand out in any pitch or workplace conversation.

Creating Impossible Moments

In magic and mentalism, I take empowerment even further. I'm not just helping people believe in dormant talents; I'm helping them believe in possibilities they don't even know exist.

Great magic experiences bypass logic and hit us straight in the heart. To create truly incredible moments, I must captivate a person's imagination and suspend their disbelief long enough to open up the possibility that maybe *(just maybe)* there's more to life than what they see, and more to discover about who they can become.

This is one of the many reasons why I fell in love with magic and mentalism, because it's the ultimate form of empowerment. When someone experiences something that defies their understanding of reality, they don't just walk away amazed. They walk away changed. That transformation is unparalleled.

This is what influence really means to me: not manipulation or performance, but presence and connection. And creating moments that feel – even for just a second – impossible to forget.

I want to create that feeling in every workshop, every conversation, every moment when someone says "I can't". Because when you help someone experience what they thought was impossible, you don't just change their mind – you dismantle the limits they've placed on themselves and help them rewrite their story.

This is not only where real connection lives, it's also where real leadership lives. Not in asking: *What can these people do for me?* That's narcissistic leadership. Real leaders ask:

How can I help this person become the absolute best version of themselves?

Because when you've experienced that transformation yourself – when you've felt the power of someone's belief expand your own potential – you develop a unique skill: the ability to spot the gap between who someone is right now, and who they could become. You learn to see their magic before they do.

Real empowerment isn't about getting people to do what you want. It's about helping others become who they're truly meant to be. Seeing them, supporting them, championing them, and believing in them before they even believe in themselves.

5 TRUTH BOMBS

Belief is contagious
When you see someone's potential before they can see it themselves, something shifts and they start believing it too.

"I trust you" are three magic words
This single phrase can quickly dissolve someone's self-doubt and transform their relationship with their own capabilities.

You can't give what you don't own
Do you want to empower others? Start by believing in yourself first. You can't give someone confidence if you haven't yet claimed it for yourself.

Recognition changes everything
One genuine acknowledgement, even a short moment of truly *seeing* someone else, can be the turning point that changes their entire life trajectory.

Empowerment multiplies influence
Help someone discover their own magic and watch what happens... Your impact doesn't just grow; it explodes.

5 QUICK WINS
(TO DO RIGHT NOW)

The character switch
Is fear blocking you? Create an alter ego who's fearless of this exact thing. Give them a name. Give them swagger. Then step into that character and attempt the task as they would, instead of as yourself. This bypasses your analytical brain's resistance and opens up new possibilities through the power of play.

Spotlight their talent
Ask someone: "What are you incredible at that you never talk about?" Then watch them light up when you give them permission to own it.

The fearless day
What would you do today if you *absolutely knew* you couldn't fail at anything? Take one step towards this.

The surprise text
Right now, pull out your phone. Text someone one specific thing you genuinely admire about them. And hit send before you overthink it.

Your mirror of truth
Ask three people you trust: "What do you see as my greatest strengths?" Then be quiet and gracefully receive what they say (without deflecting).

CHAPTER FOUR
SIGNALS
The Secret Language Of Non-Verbals

Picture this: You're standing inside Facebook's headquarters in Silicon Valley. Security to your left. Communications guy to your right. And you're about to get a private tour of the most powerful social media empire on earth. (Side note: This was 2013, when Facebook was *the* platform to be on; not just a place where boomers share blurry photos.)

The communications guy looks you straight in the eye. "Were you outside Mark's house last night?"

Your heart slams against your ribs. Your face burns red-hot. Your voice shoots up three octaves as you stammer, "No… I have no idea where he lives." And even though you're telling the absolute truth, you sound guilty as hell.

That's what happened to me during my Zucker Up adventure – a 12-day quest from Melbourne to Silicon Valley to try to make Mark Zuckerberg laugh with my best five minutes of Facebook jokes.

Mission: Make Mark Zuckerberg Laugh

Through my journey as a stand-up comedian, I discovered that creativity connects us and laughter transcends everything, building bridges between complete strangers. So I thought: if I can use creativity and humour to connect with anyone in the world, who would it be?

I set my sights on Mark Zuckerberg – the founder of the platform responsible for years of procrastination and my misguided belief that everybody cared about my daily breakfast. Let's just say I turned way too many meals into serious photo shoots.

My mission, which I called "Zucker Up", was wildly unrealistic: travel more than 16,000 kilometres from Melbourne to Dallas, to New York City, and then to Silicon Valley to make him laugh.

I knew I couldn't just rock up like a regular tech fan. I had to stand out.

So I created a giant Facebook Like costume; the first of its kind. Made entirely from neoprene (wetsuit material) to withstand winter weather on the streets of NYC, the costume was huge, heavy, and needed its own suitcase. It covered my entire body. When I wore it, the only body parts you could see were my head, hands, and lower legs.

Sounds like a dream, right? I mean, who doesn't want to dress up as a giant thumb in a foreign country?

The journey was everything I had hoped for. I stopped at the Dallas Digital Summit, where I met Apple's co-founder Steve Wozniak, who enthusiastically recorded a video wishing me good luck for the quest. I met Founder and CEO of Zuckerberg Media, Randi Zuckerberg (Mark's sister), and I met Susan Bennett, the original voice of Siri on the iPhone. For a social media geek like I was back in 2013, it was absolutely incredible.

I performed stand-up comedy sets detailing my quest at three different clubs across New York City, I hit Times Square for video vox pops asking people if Mark would like my outfit, and I documented every step online. I picked up plenty of supporters along the way.

Then, on Day 10, I arrived at Facebook's headquarters. When I saw the famous Like sign, I pulled up and froze. Suddenly, I wasn't this bold, confident social media comedian. I was one woman. Alone. In a rental car. Panicking.

I drove into the car park and freaked out. *What am I doing? Am I even allowed to be here? Is this private property?*

So I did what any millennial would do in a moment of existential crisis: I picked up my phone and checked in on Facebook, saying 'I HAVE ARRIVED!' – not revealing any of the dread and panic I was actually feeling.

I took a few deep breaths and came up with a plan: put on the giant Like costume. Ask someone where Mark's office is. Trust that Californians really are as friendly as everyone says.

I popped open the boot… stared down at my costume… and I froze again. *I can't do this. They're going to hate me. What if I get sued for copyright infringement?* The fear was overwhelming, so I got back in the car and sat in the driver's seat for 30 minutes, having an internal meltdown. It was the most fear I had ever felt. But because I had been promoting this non-stop for weeks across Facebook, I had no option but to move ahead. Terrified, and with trembling hands, I pulled the costume out of my boot, took a big deep breath, and finally shoved it over my head.

The Magic Of Embodied Confidence

That's when the magic started.

Staff began waving, laughing, and asking for photos. I was told my picture made it onto Facebook's intranet. I kept asking, "Is Mark here?" but nobody answered directly. One lovely person suggested I come back the next morning between 8 am and 9 am when everyone would be arriving for work.

So the next morning, I stood in front of the Like sign for close to an hour, and I snapped my all-time favourite photo: dressed as a giant Like, next to the giant Like sign. Children on school buses cheered. Cars honked. People took photos.

In that costume, I felt powerful, confident, unmistakably me… And then someone approached.

The Moment Everything Changed

"I'm the comms guy. What's going on?"

I launched excitedly into my story, detailing my quest from Melbourne, my goal to make Mark laugh, my love of Facebook, and my niche of writing and performing social media comedy.

"Look, Mark's away on vacation," he began. "And we have a really good relationship with the Menlo Park police, and they've said that a giant Like is a distraction to the people driving past, so…" And with Californian politeness, he suggested I wrap it up.

"Can I at least have a tour?" I pleaded.

He hesitated. "We don't normally do this… but you've come all this way. So, OK. But no photos. And leave your costume in the car."

I very happily placed the costume back in the boot and walked inside. I signed in on a tablet (super fancy and flashy in 2013) and security handed me a visitor's pass. For a moment, I was flying… *OMG, this is the best thing in the world! I've made it inside Facebook's headquarters!*

Then the communications guy got a call. He turned away for a moment. Then he turned back and looked me straight in the eye.

"Were you outside Mark's house last night?"

The Incongruence Disaster

What happened next was a masterclass in how your body can betray you – even when you're telling the truth.

Within moments, security plucked the pass out of my hand and I was completely thrown off balance. I froze. My whole body shifted. My face got red-hot. My voice went up three octaves and became shaky and defensive. My breathing got shallow. Adrenaline flooded my system.

"No… I have no idea where he lives."

And even though I was telling the absolute truth, every single physiological response screamed "suspicious behaviour". I wasn't congruent, I wasn't grounded, and I wasn't standing in my power.

Within minutes I was escorted off the property. Security accompanied me to my car and watched as I drove away.

The Devastating Truth About Influence

Because I wasn't anchored in my own power, I looked guilty. When you're incongruent – when your words say one thing but your body says another – it's palpable. People feel it. They sense the disconnect. And in high-stakes moments, that disconnect reads as deception, even when you're telling the absolute truth.

I was escorted out of Facebook's headquarters not because of evidence of wrongdoing but because of my body, my voice, and my energy. If I'd stayed calm, grounded, and connected to my message, the whole interaction could have been different.

The Silent Language We All Speak

That Facebook experience taught me something crucial: Before you say a single word, your body has already told the room a story.

How you enter. How you hold your shoulders. The tilt of your head. The sparkle (or lack thereof) in your eyes. The tempo of your breath. The shape of your smile. The way you gesture. You might be saying you're confident, but we see it (or don't see it) before you even open your mouth to say a single word.

The Language We Never Lost

Before we had words, we used gestures. For millennia, we have connected using non-verbal communication – eye movements, facial expressions, body language. And while civilisation has evolved, our ancient brain hasn't.

Evolutionary psychologists say our brains are essentially "stone-age minds" designed to solve daily challenges faced by our hunter-gatherer ancestors.[5] Research shows, even babies can read emotional expressions before they understand words.[6]

So even though we live in a world of smartphones, touch screens, and Wi-Fi networks, non-verbal communication isn't optional – it's our first language. We were reading each other's bodies long before we had any verbal language to work with. We used this skill to survive, assess, bond, protect, and connect. It's innate. And it's still the foundation of how we connect, whether we're pitching a multimillion-dollar idea or asking for extra guacamole on our taco.

Learning To Read Physical Signals

As a magician, I've learnt that children are the hardest audiences to fool. Why? Because they see everything. They haven't unlearnt their instincts yet. They read your rhythm, sense your energy, and notice when you hesitate. If your body betrays the trick, they know instantly. And kids are brutally honest. If they think you're lying, they'll say so, without hesitation.

We all have that instinct, but as we get older, societal expectations, etiquette, and cultural norms teach us to second-guess or ignore it. We learn to override our intuition and conceal how we truly feel. In doing so, we start mistrusting the very cues we were born to read, and in some cases, we forget how to read them entirely. As a result, we get uncomfortable in our bodies. We disconnect, we doubt ourselves, and we stiffen up. We lose our natural and authentic flow in both communication and expression.

After running hundreds of public speaking workshops across Australia with participants as diverse as lawyers, executives, artists, teachers, consultants, software engineers, marketers, sales teams, social workers (and many more), I have observed that most people don't feel confident in their body when they communicate. Not from a lack of expressiveness, but because they were never taught how.

There's a faulty assumption that just because we communicate and use our bodies every day, we should automatically know how to communicate well under pressure. But expressive, powerful, and embodied communication is an art form, and like any art, it requires learning techniques and strategies, embracing a beginner's mindset, being open to new ideas, and happily making mistakes while working towards confidence.

Spotting Incongruence In Others

If your body language contradicts your message, your credibility crashes.

You might say, "That's a brilliant idea!", but if your arms and legs are crossed, and your eyes drop, we don't believe you at all. Or you might attempt your best "I'm fine" smile, but if your eyebrows say "I hate this whole situation", your face will expose the truth.

Psychologist Paul Ekman discovered seven universal micro-expressions that remain consistent across all cultures: anger, contempt, disgust, fear, happiness, sadness, and surprise.[7] These involuntary facial expressions flash across our face in just 1/25th of a second, revealing our true reaction before our conscious mind can control our expression – and before our mouth has any time to camouflage the truth. What does this tell us? Emotion is innate and it is felt, whether we vocalise it or not.

Here's how fast we judge each other: a 2006 Princeton University study showed that we form first impressions of faces in just 100 milliseconds.[8] Participants judged traits like trustworthiness and competence in 1/10th of a second; the tiniest window of time.

The Power Of True Alignment

When your words, body, voice, expression, and intention all align, you radiate clarity and conviction, and people trust you.

In hypnosis, that alignment has a name: **congruence** (more on this in Chapter 7). When someone's presence precedes their voice, that's the unspoken language of power. If even one part is out of sync, your message doesn't land. People may not be able to articulate what's off, but they'll know. And that disconnect kills trust.

Here are congruence killers that destroy credibility:

- Picking at your fingers while speaking
- Crossing your arms when expressing "openness"
- Avoiding eye contact in meaningful discussions
- Fidgeting with every object in reach

- Hunching your shoulders like you're carrying the world
- Shrinking into yourself

Each sends a mixed signal, and mixed signals confuse your audience and dilute your influence.

Your Power Toolkit

Here are some of my favourite tools, which I've developed and refined through years of performing and delivering workshops.

Glitter Chest: Instant Confidence

This is by far my favourite. I created this technique because I needed something fast, visual, and fun that anyone could do, anywhere. It's easy and profoundly effective. Just imagine glitter bursting out of your chest. Try it, right now. Imagine glitter beaming out of you in every direction.

What happens? Your chest expands. Your shoulders move backwards. As your chest opens, you hold your head higher. When you hold your head higher, your chin lifts and your eye line rises. You're now in an expansive and confident pose; open and strong, like a lion. If you're thinking this feels silly, perfect. The most powerful tools often feel ridiculous until they work.

Don't let this be a one-time experiment. For the next week, do Glitter Chest before every important conversation. Notice how differently people respond when you walk already embodying confidence, rather than hoping to find it.

If I had used Glitter Chest at Facebook and remained physically grounded when asked, "Were you outside Mark's house last night?" my energy would have been very different.

The Smile That Opens Doors

When you smile authentically, you radiate warmth and confidence, opening doors to deeper connections.

Try this experiment: Say "I'd love to discuss this opportunity with you" with a serious expression. Notice how it feels and sounds. Now say the exact same words but start with a genuine smile *before* you begin. Can you feel the difference?

We have more than 40 muscles in our face. When we smile, it sends a signal through our body saying "I'm happy", followed by a rush of feel-good chemicals. Your smile doesn't just make you more attractive – it makes your ideas more attractive. People are naturally drawn to positive energy and are more likely to say yes to someone who makes them feel good.

But authenticity is crucial. In a true Duchenne smile,[9] we lift the corners of our mouth and raise our cheeks, and this creates crow's feet wrinkles around our eyes.[10] When we do a polite (or fake) smile, only our mouth moves.

When you're fake smiling, we can tell. Your smile is your invitation to connect. Make it genuine.

Your Voice, Your Power

Your voice is your secret communication weapon. Most people speak in a limited (and boring) range, missing the power of pitch, rhythm, pacing, pausing, and inflection to captivate their audience.

When you whisper, people lean in because you've created intimacy and intrigue. When you speak with depth and authority, you command respect. When you emphasise key words, you direct attention exactly where it needs to be for your message to become precise and unforgettable. When you vary your pace from quick excitement to slow deliberation, you take people on an auditory and emotional journey. When you use strategic pauses, you sound more confident, feel more confident, and you build tension to truly let important points land. And when you change your pitch and add inflection to create rhythm and express emotion, you bring your words to life.

Our voice is one of the most under-utilised tools we have, but also the part of our physicality that gives us away the fastest. When we're under pressure, it's the hardest to control. At Facebook, my voice became shaky and high-pitched. If I had controlled my vocal presence and kept it steady, grounded, and balanced, the outcome could have been entirely different.

Your voice shapes how people receive your message. Use it intentionally.

Strategic Pauses: The Game Changer

In comedy, we call a pause a *beat*. Timing is everything when it comes to delivering a killer punchline. The same principle applies to all powerful communication. When you pause strategically, you:

- Command attention: Silence makes people lean in
- Create emphasis and anticipation: Words that follow a pause carry more weight
- Allow ideas to sink in: Pauses give your message (and your audience) space to breathe
- Project confidence: Racing or rushing signals anxiety

Most of us speak way too fast when the pressure's on. We speed up because we (incorrectly) think we need to fill every gap, and we try to escape discomfort by cramming everything in. But strategic pauses draw people in and make your words far more impactful.

So, learn to fall in love with silence in communication. Most people fear it, but silence is powerful. It creates space, commands respect, gives you room to breathe, and makes your next words land like gold.

Hands That Speak Volumes

When nervous in important conversations, we naturally fidget: shuffling papers, adjusting our watch, twisting our rings. People notice these nervous tells immediately, and they undermine our credibility.

Engaging speakers don't just talk – they animate their ideas to bring them to life and make them pop. Your hands help translate abstract concepts into something that others can see, feel, and understand. We need to gesture intentionally. An analysis of thousands of hours of TED Talks by Science of People, run by researcher and author Vanessa Van Edwards, found the most viral talks, and the most popular speakers, used nearly twice as many hand gestures as the least popular ones.[11]

Choose your most important points and use your hands to help bring those points to life. When your gestures align with your key messages, your words have more impact and your audience stays engaged.

Your hands are powerful tools for influence.

Eye Contact: Your Lightning-Fast Connection

In our digitally distracting world, eye contact helps us connect, quickly.

When you truly see people, rather than just scanning them, or staring at your notes, you create instant connections. Eye contact signals that you're fully present and engaged, making people feel valued and heard – a foundational element of influence. So what's the sweet spot? Long enough to connect; brief enough to avoid the creepy zone. Research shows we're most comfortable with eye contact lasting 3.3 seconds (with a range of two to five seconds).[12]

Try this: In your next conversation, maintain deliberate eye contact for three-to-five-second intervals. Notice how it impacts the quality of connection.

Eye contact isn't just looking; it's connecting. Make it count.

The Magic Is In The Alignment

When you use your body as a powerful tool for connection, everything changes. Your influence skyrockets. You become someone people *feel*, someone whose messages land, and someone who moves people because every part of you is saying the same thing.

That Facebook experience taught me this lesson the hard way: it's not just what you say – it's how your entire body says it.

When your words, tone, physical expression, and intention align, you radiate trust and confidence. And people don't just hear your words; they feel your energy. And that energy either works for you or against you.

The failure at Facebook wasn't getting escorted off the property. The real failure would have been letting that incongruence stop me from trying again, from learning, and from becoming more aligned in every interaction that followed.

Because when you master the silent language of power – when every part of you speaks the same truth – you don't just communicate differently. You transform how people experience you. You walk into rooms and shift the energy. You build trust without trying. And your impact lingers long after you've gone.

5 TRUTH BOMBS

Your body speaks before you do
Before you say a single word, your posture, energy, and presence have already told the room everything.

Posture changes everything
Strike an open and expansive Glitter Chest pose and feel the confidence kick in.

Congruence builds trust
When your words say one thing but your body says another, we believe your body every single time.

Silence is your secret weapon
Strategic pauses don't just create space. They make your next words land with absolute power.

Alignment creates instant belief
When your words, energy, and body all point in the same direction, people don't *decide* to trust you. They just do.

5 QUICK WINS
(TO DO RIGHT NOW)

The Glitter Chest challenge
Right now, imagine glitter exploding from your chest. Feel what happens: your chest opens, your shoulders move back, and your chin lifts. Notice how this instantly changes your energy (and makes you smile).

The eye-smile test
Look in the mirror and do a fake "Joker" smile (a mouth-only grin). Now smile with everything you've got, lifting your cheeks and crinkling the muscles on the sides of your eyes. Feel that difference? That's what authenticity looks like.

The pause that commands
Before your next big point, add a deliberate three-second pause. Hold this silence and watch every head turn toward you.

Read the room without words
Pick one person in your next conversation. Don't listen to their words; instead, watch their body language, their posture, and their expressions. See what story their body is telling you.

Lock eyes to build trust
In your next conversation, make an effort to create meaningful eye contact. Notice how the energy between you and the other person changes.

CHAPTER FIVE
EXPRESSION
The Secret Of Language That Opens Minds

Back in 2014, I did something unbelievably stupid: I put a giant raw egg in my mouth for a social media video.

And not just any egg – an extra-large, farm-fresh, completely uncooked egg that I was convinced would launch me to internet stardom. In my mind, this wasn't just content creation, this was art. I genuinely believed my "genius idea" would become a viral masterpiece sitting somewhere between Steven Spielberg and Quentin Tarantino-level brilliance; a cinematic triumph.

I was wrong. So very wrong. Little did I know this one dumb, poorly thought-out, highly questionable life choice would turn my world completely upside down and eventually teach me an unforgettable lesson about the power of language.

When Viral Dreams Go Wrong

My time as a stand-up comedian was a period when YouTube

stars were emerging and soaring to never-before-seen levels of internet fame. Deep inside, I had burning aspirations to join their ranks.

At the time, Twitter had a short-form video app called Vine which turned everyday content creators into viral megastars through six-second clips that played on loop… and I wanted to be one of them.

Wouldn't it look hilarious if I start a Vine video with an egg in my mouth, and at the end of the clip, there's yolk splashed all over the sink? The video would loop seamlessly: egg cracking in my mouth, yolk spilling into the sink, back and forth, back and forth.

I'd like to point out, whatever your reaction is to that visual, trust me, in hindsight, I'm feeling it too. If it's not already clear, I use the words "genius idea" with a great level of sarcasm. Looking back, I cannot for the life of me see any solid humour in this short-form video concept.

The Injury That Changed Everything

I grab an extra-large raw egg from the fridge. (Because why would you buy any other size?) I carefully wedge the egg in my mouth and tightly purse my lips around it to keep it in place. I hold the egg carton up in one hand and my iPhone up in the other, totally living the Hollywood dream: directing and starring in my very own mini-movie in my bathroom.

However, as soon as I push record, I feel this piercing, shooting pain all the way up the right side of my head, and down my neck. It's so painful that I stop recording immediately and, in an instant, my Academy Award-winning dream is crushed.

Annoyed and angry, I delete the micro-seconds of footage and forcefully throw the egg in the bin, never to speak of this incident again… or so I think.

That weekend, I went to a party with friends. One of my friends was cracking jokes and I was laughing hysterically – the type of laughter where every burst is accompanied by tears of joy. It sounds brilliant, right?

Well… yes and no. Every time she made me laugh, a super sharp pain hit my cheeks. I would laugh, then a few seconds later feel an electric radiating pain across my face. By the end of the night, every time I laughed, I was squeezing my face with both hands in an attempt to, unsuccessfully, stop the sheer agony.

The next morning, I woke up with a headache from hell. It felt like I'd been knocked in the head with a ton of bricks from every angle. My cheeks were swollen and my jaw muscles were red and hot. Something wasn't right.

I went to the dentist, explaining this very random series of events. "Well, I put an egg in my mouth for a social media video…" He looked at me, perplexed. At first he laughed, because why would anyone do that, right? After a long pause, he said: "You've overstretched your jaw ligament. Go on anti-inflammatories for six weeks. If it doesn't settle down, we'll send you to a TMJ specialist." I discovered TMJ – the temporomandibular joint – connects our jaw to our skull and is the most powerful joint in our whole body. Yet, apparently, it can get injured by biting too hard on a boiled lolly, accidentally chewing on an olive pip, and, believe it or not, shoving whole raw eggs in your mouth.

So began my medical marathon. TMJ Specialist #1 prescribed medication and strict guidelines: only eat soft foods, put hot towels on your face three times daily, and "only yawn halfway". Translation: no bread crusts, no steaks, no raw carrots, no almonds, no chips, no chewy caramel. Basically, eliminate all foods that require teeth.

Living With Cruel Irony

An MRI showed that my two jaw discs were not sitting in the correct position. Every time I laughed, I experienced intense agony. The craziest part was the irony: I became the comedian who couldn't laugh and the speaker who couldn't speak. The very thing that brought me joy now also brought immense pain. And the very tools I'd built my life around: my voice, my words, my humour – now caused me agony.

What followed was 15 months of medical ping-pong. Different specialists and practitioners promising hope, each delivering temporary relief at best. And the pattern remained: laughter, pain, headaches; laughter, pain, headaches.

At every opportunity, I avoided anything that might make me smile. To be someone whose job was to bring joy to others while being unable to physically express joy myself – without insane pain – felt like a cruel impossibility.

The most difficult moment came during what should have been one of my greatest professional triumphs. I was delivering a keynote presentation on creativity and launching my first book. There was a huge line of people waiting to meet me. What should have been pure excitement – my first book signing – became absolute agony.

Between the presentation and book signing, I had to disappear to massage my cheeks. I needed that break to handle the speaking and smiling required. I kept running to the bathroom to put cream on my face. I was trying to engage and be friendly while barely moving my cheeks – smiling only at the exact moment a selfie was taken. And after every smile, the radiating pain compounded my killer headache. When people congratulated me, all I felt was sadness. *Why am I in such pain during what should be such a happy time?*

The contrast was stark: professional success coupled with personal torture. The pain affected everything: my focus, my precision, the energy I brought to events, and my ability to create the experiences people deserved. I had lost all hope of finding lasting relief.

Three Words Of Hope

Then one day, I walked into a vocal physiotherapist's office. I was nervous to see yet another new practitioner, because trust was a huge factor. With so much pain, I was reluctant to let another set of hands work on my condition.

I walked in already feeling defeated, both wired and exhausted by my own anxiety. But the physiotherapist was kind, gentle, and cautious with her words. She was also really upbeat. She asked me questions to determine where I was at, mentally and physically, and then she looked me straight in the eye with absolute conviction and said something that completely surprised me – something no one had said to me during my months of agony:

"You will heal."

I froze.

Wait… what?

Her voice was calm, clear, and absolutely certain:

"You. Will. Heal."

Until that moment, all I'd heard was ***won't, can't, shouldn't***. This was different. Her tone, her body language, her sincerity – she believed it 100%. My immediate reaction was shock. But she had so much conviction, there was no room for any other possibility.

Even though I didn't completely believe her, intuitively, her words resonated with me. She became my beacon of hope, and for the first time there was optimism from her certainty. The heaviness I had carried cracked open and I got a glimpse of a future without pain.

In that moment, I realised something profound: words don't just describe reality – they shape it. Her language had created a bridge from limitation to possibility that no previous medical diagnosis or practitioner had offered.

The Power Of "Imagine"

Language precision became essential in my public speaking workshops, where I discovered one of the most powerful words to counteract resistance: *Imagine*.

Most people are deeply uncomfortable talking about their strengths. We're taught to stay small and let others shine. In Australia, Tall Poppy Syndrome makes it worse – we celebrate people until they succeed, then tear them down. So when I ask workshop participants to share why they're awesome, I regularly hit a wall of resistance.

Instead, people are overly enthusiastic to profess that they have impostor syndrome. It's almost become the new badge of honour. Often in my workshops, I'll ask: "Who feels they have impostor syndrome?" Hands shoot up without hesitation. **Why are we so happy to highlight there's something wrong with us instead of celebrating what's right?** People prefer to focus on what they don't believe they do well, and identify the skills they think they're missing, instead of focusing on what's actually there – and what's actually true.

But in public speaking, you need to own your awesomeness. If you don't own every part of why you're brilliant and incredible and amazing, how can you share your message powerfully? You need conviction about why you're the best person to deliver your message, *right now*. Because if you don't believe it, why would I or anyone else believe it?

So I discovered a way around this using one simple word: *Imagine*. I play a game with workshop participants when their resistance overwhelms them. I say: "Just imagine… Just imagine that you are a different version of yourself right now, and this version is happy and confident and just loves public speaking. Can you play a game of imagination with me?"

They hesitantly say yes.

This language changes everything because it gets them out of the fixed model of their existing reality and into a playful space. Then I say: "Just imagine that you're about to give a presentation, and that you love giving presentations. And imagine that the highlight of your colleagues' week is listening to your presentation. Can you imagine that? Can you stay with me? Can you keep playing? Amazing. How would you open your presentation?"

This simple game activates their imagination, and they go on to tell me confidently and eloquently exactly how they would address the room.

Here's what happened with one woman in a recent workshop. Despite all of her colleagues clearly loving and respecting her, she couldn't acknowledge anything positive about herself. It felt too foreign, too uncomfortable. Every attempt to discuss her strengths was met with pushback.

But when I asked her to imagine she was someone else – someone who happened to look exactly like her but was confident and powerful – everything shifted. Her face lit up. She started smiling. It became easy. Most importantly, it felt better in her body than the full-on resistance she'd been carrying.

"This version of me," she said, now animated, "speaks three different languages and loves cooking and dancing. She's playful and sees the best in others. She has an amazing network of friends and colleagues, and is really good at developing relationships. She loves travelling the world and is grateful for everything she has. She's thoughtful, caring, ambitious, and always goes over and above."

In that moment, a sense of wonder opens up, and their true power comes through. They shine because they don't feel trapped by their current identity. As adults, we're so fixed in our patterns, thoughts and behaviours, that we often stick to behaviour that doesn't serve us, or help us grow, simply because it's what we've always done…

Play opens a powerful door. I watched the light in her eyes return. Her face softened, her shoulders dropped, her defences were down, and within minutes, *imagine* had done what months of coaching couldn't. The transformation wasn't just in what she said – it was in where her confidence was coming from. Instead of seeking external approval to feel confident, she was expressing from her own authentic power. The source had changed from outside-in to inside-out confidence.

The Wrong Words

Language precision is also critical in magic and mentalism. If I don't use exactly the right words to guide a volunteer through an effect, the trick fails. Every single word choice matters.

I learnt this the hard way during a keynote for 250 people. My volunteer on stage kept saying, "Another trick, another trick, another trick" after each effect, trying to expose the tricks rather than enjoy them. Distracted by her attitude, I muddled my verbal instructions and several effects failed.

The most incredible part of performing magic is helping people suspend disbelief, and truly believe in wonder. But once they see the cracks in an illusion, you can't bring them back to that pure sense of awe. So at this event, I failed my audience. Promising magical moments and then watching them fall apart because of imprecise language was gut-wrenching.

That experience taught me two critical lessons: First, never select magic volunteers – always let them volunteer themselves. Second, be meticulous with every instruction. My banter is always spontaneous, but the words guiding each magic and mentalism effect must be absolutely precise.

Power Language Tools

I've learnt some amazing language tools through hypnosis, neuro-linguistic programming (NLP), and my own pursuit of self-development, that serve as constant reminders in my life – ways to create possibility instead of limitation, and to see new opportunities instead of staying trapped in habitual patterns. I want to share the most powerful and empowering tools I've discovered. Tools that will help not only you, but everyone you connect with.

Language That Assumes Success

Presuppositions are a powerful verbal technique used in hypnosis. When you 'presuppose', you're assuming positive outcomes and guiding a person there. It's empowering language because you're talking about what *will* happen, and not what *won't* happen. When it's done right, it fuels our confidence and fills us with possibility, leaving no room for negative outcomes.

For example, instead of asking, "How will you feel if you climb Mt. Fuji?" – which gives someone room for doubt – I would instead ask, "How will you feel when you're standing at the top of Mt. Fuji with the sun rising behind you?" This presupposition plants the seed that success is inevitable, and not optional.

Now, I use "when" instead of "if" constantly.

Remember how we talked about believing in someone before they believe in themselves? This is where presuppositions become your secret empowerment weapon. When you believe in someone's potential, your language becomes the bridge to their transformation. Instead of "If you get confident enough to present…" you say, "When you step into your power and present, how does it feel?" You're not just using different words – you're setting them up to expect success by using language that assumes their transformation is already underway.

Building Instant Rapport

Mirroring a person's language is another valuable tool from hypnosis. If someone says, "What I really need is clarity", don't say, "So you want direction". Say, "Let's get you that clarity". By reflecting their exact words back, they feel heard, seen, and valued, instantly.

In recognising our own language patterns being mirrored back to us, we think: "This person gets me." It creates immediate trust and connection because you're speaking their own dialogue, and not translating it into your own words. (Bonus: This form of listening forces us to pay more attention and be more present.)

Language Swaps that Open Minds

We often use language without thinking about how deeply it cuts others and how detrimental it might be to our own potential. Here are six powerful language swaps to open minds instead of shut down possibilities.

Add "Yet" To Transform Limitations

"I can't do public speaking."
"I can't talk to my boss about that."
"I can't start my own business."

"I can't" is a brick wall, with nowhere to move. And most of the time it's not even true. It usually means "I'm scared"… just dressed up in different words. The solution is to add one powerful word that changes everything: *yet*.

"I can't present confidently... *yet*."
"I can't launch my own business... *yet*."

That tiny word opens the door to growth and creates possibility where before there was only finality.

Replace "But" With "And"

"I had a great presentation... but I stumbled."

The word "but" is like a whiteboard eraser. It completely eliminates whatever came before it, forcing us to focus only on the limitation.

When you replace "but" with "and" it means both things become simultaneously true and valid:

"I had a great presentation *and* I stumbled."

Stop Diluting Your Power

"I'm just learning..."
"I'm not really an expert..."
"I'm only trying to help..."

This language takes your power away. Instead, own what you're doing:

"I'm *learning* a new skill."
"I'm *developing* expertise."
"I'm *helping* in a meaningful way."

When you speak in alignment with your growth and forward momentum, it empowers you.

Change "Should" To "Choose"

"I should be more confident."
"I should be further along."

"Should" is shame in disguise, filled with a heavy sense of guilt that weighs us down. Changing this word to "choose" creates empowering statements and declarations.

"I *choose* to build confidence."
"I *choose* to make epic progress."

Swap "Hope" For "Committed"

"I hope I get the job."
"I hope they like my presentation."

Hope works for wishes, but using it in everyday statements surrenders your power to external circumstances. Instead, own your commitment:

"I'm *committed* to landing this job or something better."

"I'm *committed* to trusting myself."

One creates anxiety. The other creates grounded confidence.

Transform "Trying" Into "Becoming"

"Try" sets us up for failure through language alone. When I say, "Try to guess the answer to this riddle", my assumption is that you'll give it a shot, but you'll be unsuccessful.

When we say "becoming", we step into possibility:

"I'm *becoming* someone who speaks with confidence."

"I'm *becoming* someone who backs myself completely."

Why Your Words Matter

The path from that ridiculous egg video to understanding the precision of language wasn't linear by any means. It took chronic pain, medical marathons, and hundreds of workshops to understand the truth I had experienced in that physiotherapist's office: Words don't just describe reality; they shape it.

I've learnt that certain words open minds and create possibilities, while others shut down our potential, and the potential of others. As a result, I've removed the word "can't" from my vocabulary entirely. And if I do catch myself saying it, I very quickly correct it.

My physiotherapist's words didn't heal my physical condition, but her language gave me something more powerful: a new perspective on my reality. When I learnt to say, "As I find new ways to navigate this condition", instead of "Will this pain ever end?", everything shifted. I stopped entertaining victimhood and started focusing on healing, resilience, and growth.

When you master these language tools, everything changes. You don't just communicate differently – you connect differently, you lead differently, and you influence differently. Your words are powerful because they don't just carry meaning. They shape what's possible – for you and others.

5 TRUTH BOMBS

Words don't just describe reality: they create it
The language you choose has the power to rewire how people think, feel, and act in real time.

"Imagine" is your resistance killer
This single word bypasses defensive walls and opens minds to new possibilities in a powerful and playful way.

Swap "if" for "when" and watch what happens
The moment you stop questioning whether something will happen and start planning for success, your entire mindset changes.

Tiny word swaps, massive shifts
Replace "but" with "and" to keep possibilities open. Replace "should" with "choose" to replace guilt with power.

Your breaking point becomes your breakthrough
The struggles that nearly break us always hold the most powerful lessons.

5 QUICK WINS
(TO DO RIGHT NOW)

Swap "if" for "when"
Stop saying "If I achieve this". Start saying "When I achieve this". Your brain and body hear and feel the difference.

Add "yet" to (almost) everything
How often do you catch yourself saying "I can't"? The answer is to add one powerful word: "yet". Feel how that tiny word cracks any limitation wide open.

Replace "but" with "and"
The next three times you say "but", switch it to "and". Watch how it stops erasing what came before, and starts building possibilities instead.

Practice possibility language
In one conversation this week, replace two limiting phrases: Turn "I'll try" into "I'm becoming"; and turn "I hope" into "I'm committed to". Notice how it makes you feel.

Catch your critic
Track your self-talk for one day. Every time you hear "I can't", "I'm not good at", or "I always mess up", write it down. At the end of the day, you'll have your top three negative phrases. Next step: Flip them around to reframe them into power statements.

CHAPTER SIX
NAVIGATE

The Secret Of Meeting Hearts Before Moving Minds

I was backstage, looking over my 10 killer opening jokes, when I heard the sirens.

Someone had collapsed during afternoon tea. An ambulance was called and there was chaos everywhere. In 20 minutes, I was supposed to deliver a high-energy keynote to wake up the crowd for the final conference session of the day.

This moment mattered. It was one of the first events I had done with this particular agent. It was the first time I'd ever worked with this client. And I knew this event was a big deal for their delegates, with the entire regional area coming together for their annual event.

As a speaker, I am always at conferences, but those attending have invested money and time away from work, and it's a very special occasion.

I peeked from backstage. The energy in the room was

stagnant. Tension was palpable. No one knew what to do or what to say, and I saw a stillness I'll never forget. There was a mixture of fear and confusion on people's faces and their bodies were stiff. The room was quiet, and they had lost their joy and buoyancy.

Meanwhile, I'm standing there with my perfectly crafted opening and my brain is spinning. *Do I acknowledge what just happened? Or do I pretend everything's fine?*

The comedian in me who just wants to entertain and break the ice, really wanted to say the jokes. But the professional speaker in me knew I needed to connect with the audience exactly where they were. And in my heart, I knew I needed to be respectful – someone in that audience could have been the sister, brother, mother, father, cousin, work colleague, or boss of the person attended to by the ambulance. Their fate was still unknown.

Standing in those wings, I made a choice that changed everything.

The Charity Event I'll Never Forget

Rewind to three years earlier, and I was completely different on stage. I would have charged forward with my planned material regardless of what the room needed. I used to be someone who was so focused on leading people exactly where I wanted them to go, that I never stopped to see where they actually were.

The breaking point came at what should have been a simple stand-up comedy gig. I was asked to do a charity event. I knew it wasn't the right audience, but the organiser insisted. And I felt an obligation because they were raising funds for an important not-for-profit organisation: "Social media and technology is something we need to learn about. It will be really dynamic and exciting," they told me.

It was intimate. Me and 20 people. So small we didn't even need a microphone.

Every joke met silence. Every punchline drew blank stares. They weren't aggressive like the cruise passengers; just mostly confused and concerned.

All I had was social media material at that stage, and I was mortified, standing there watching people who weren't even trying to politely laugh. They didn't understand and I could see it in their eyes: *We feel sorry for you. We want to laugh, but we don't know what you're talking about.*

The worst part? I knew it was wrong before I walked in. I told them I wasn't the right fit, but they were raising money for charity so I wanted to help. But I quickly lost the entire room, and there was nothing I could do.

If that happened now, I'd stop mid-set and say, "OK, cool. Clearly not the right fit. But you'll love me anyway because now I'll give you some time back." But I didn't have that confidence then.

So I stood there, delivering jokes to people who didn't understand the intricacies of iPhone apps, social media platforms, or the tech I was talking about. And then I had to make awkward small talk afterwards.

Living With The Pattern Of Disconnection

During my Melbourne Fringe Festival run, I rode the highest highs and lowest lows. This festival is tough for a comedian. It's a mixed arts festival, unlike the Melbourne International Comedy Festival, where everyone attending shows already has a strong comedy appetite. Some nights I'd finish my Fringe show thinking, *I can't do this anymore. I can't get up tomorrow night.* Not because they didn't enjoy it – they loved the show, and it was successful – but the tiniest thing could derail the energy. A mobile phone. Someone's sideways glance. Spontaneous banter gone wrong. It could all collapse in seconds.

At that time, I was so externally oriented, judging my self-worth by laughs I could see and hear. I expected certain responses and when I didn't get them, I panicked. I'd spiral into assumptions about what went wrong.

I remember calling a friend, a comedian who lives in NYC. "I can't do this anymore," I said, almost crying.

"What do you mean?" she asked

"It was the worst show, even though it was amazing," I explained.

"Ha ha, that's comedy," she said. "High highs, low lows. Tomorrow night will be brilliant, and you'll love it all over again. Don't give up."

Even off stage, I made the same mistakes. When pitching social media packages to dentists in the early years of consulting, I didn't meet them where they were. I created packages based on what I believed they needed as a potential client, never really considering what they actually wanted or what was feasible.

So that night at the charity event, I made a promise to myself: no more events unless the audience is absolutely the right fit. Don't just do it because it's a *nice* thing to do or the *right* thing to do – because no matter what my intentions might be, if the content is not the right fit, it will be terrible for everyone. But making that promise and actually knowing how to connect with the right audience? Those were two completely different things…

Turning Disruption Into Connection

The breakthrough came years later at a corporate conference, in the most unexpected way.

After years of comedy, I had learnt to love hecklers. My philosophy is: if you have the energy and audacity to dish it out to me, I will happily serve it back.

My keynote presentations are always very high energy. I jump on and off the stage, and they're super-interactive, with a lot of engaging audience discussions. At this conference, I encountered my very first corporate heckler – the company's class clown, who was determined to steal the spotlight. So, I met him exactly where he was: craving attention and centre stage. I played along briefly with some banter as he kept serving up smart-arse remarks, but I soon realised he was not going to back down. He loved every second of being the star. So, I gave him exactly what he wanted. I handed him the microphone and said: "You've got two minutes. It's all yours. Say whatever you want, then sit down so I can continue."

His colleagues erupted in supportive laughter and cheers. And he said just a few short words before happily handing the mic back.

That moment revealed something important: when you truly meet someone where they are – even when it's disruptive – you can lead them (and everyone else) exactly where you need to go. By meeting his need for attention, I led the entire room back to connection and laughter.

Acknowledging The Awkward

This skill didn't come naturally. Stand-up comedy taught me to acknowledge the awkward, which means if something is happening in the room and the audience is distracted by it, I can't pretend I haven't seen it. I must meet them in that shared distraction before I can lead them anywhere else.

Acknowledging the awkward has saved me countless times. During a workshop once, a bird smashed into the window. I was stunned. The whole concept of a bird smashing into a window is bizarre. I said, "Did that actually just happen, or did I hallucinate for a moment?" Everyone started laughing, and it ended up creating an instant connection that diffused a very unusual situation. We all united in a shared experience, and the spontaneous humour that emerged was far funnier than anything planned or scripted.

I do this constantly at corporate events. If a mobile phone goes off, I'll say mid-sentence: "Whose mobile phone was that? Did you not get the memo to put it on silent?" I'll jump off the stage and into the audience, scanning the crowd. "Where are you? Where are you?" One person is often scrambling in their bag or pocket, hunched over, while everyone around them points. "Can we just get you to stand up, please? Let's give you a round of applause!"

I turn it into this hysterical moment where the phone owner is laughing, everyone else is laughing, and there's a clear implied lesson: turn your phone off if you haven't already, or you'll be next.

Meeting Students In Their Fear

In public speaking workshops, I meet students directly in their fear by sharing my personal disasters first.

I show a photo from my first-ever set at the New York Comedy Club. "Do I look cool, calm, and relaxed?" I tell the truth: that I was terrified, that I had memorised everything (which I never recommend), and when I delivered my first joke, I completely froze (more on this in Chapter 7).

I share a screenshot from my first TV interview, where my face was bright red despite having heaps of makeup on. To this day, I can't remember anything about the experience because I was so nervous. I don't remember the flight to Sydney, I don't remember recording, and I don't remember what I said. Nerves completely took over.

I tell the Facebook story because the anxiety before putting on that costume was hands-down the scariest 30 minutes of my life.

And I also share the story of one of my earliest keynote presentations when I was so nervous that I didn't sleep for one second the night before – tossing and turning, tossing and turning, thinking, *I need to sleep. Why can't I sleep? 1am, 2am, 3am, 4am. Better get up and have a coffee!*

I do this because I meet them in their fear and concern: "Whatever you're feeling, I've been there. I've felt that fear a million times over and I know exactly what you're experiencing. I thought I would die too, but guess what? I survived, I learnt how to get through it, and I even made the process really fun! And now I'm here to share those lessons with you."

I meet them where they are, then transform their resistance into a shared experience. This is so important because if I just said, "Do this, do that", they wouldn't trust I fully understand their worries and they wouldn't believe me.

The Masters Of Meeting First

The best communicators intuitively understand you can't lead someone unless you first meet them. And some of the best podcasters in the world make this look effortless.

Steven Bartlett (*The Diary Of A CEO*) meets his guests by syncing to their pace – pausing when they pause, breathing with them, and holding silence so they have time to share their ideas. And he also meets his listeners by bringing them up to speed with clarifying questions for guests even when he already knows the answers. He leads both sides into complete clarity.

Lewis Howes (*The School of Greatness*) meets guests in story, often inviting them to revisit pivotal early moments – before the success, before they knew how it would turn out. Because he shares his own vulnerability, they feel safe exploring those spaces with him. From that shared ground, he leads with bold questions that push towards breakthrough moments.

Mel Robbins (*The Mel Robbins Podcast*) meets with intimacy, using inclusive language like "your buddy Mel". This places her shoulder-to-shoulder with her listeners. By naming her own struggles and truths first, she meets people in their challenges, then leads them towards action and motivation with tough-love empowerment.

Jay Shetty (*On Purpose*) meets through empathy, not authority, showing up as the curious and connected student, sharing his own struggles and experiences with complete honesty. That openness creates instant trust. From that meeting point, he gently guides guests into vulnerable places they might never have explored, leading both guests and listeners towards deeper insights.

And in her TED Talks, academic, author and researcher Brené Brown doesn't just lecture about vulnerability. She meets her audiences in their own shame and honesty, and then leads them, gently, towards courage.

In their own unique ways, they each show that true influence requires both meeting and leading.

Know Your Audience First

This approach goes deeper than what NLP teaches as "pace and lead" – matching someone's behaviour before guiding them somewhere new. Meeting people means connecting emotionally, energetically, and intellectually. We step into their world: What's weighing them down? What lights them up? Where do they want to go, and what's blocking them?

To create meaningful connections, we must meet every audience where they are. And this kind of meeting doesn't start when I walk on stage. It starts the moment I accept the booking.

Ever since the cruise ship, I have been diligent about understanding my audience. For every keynote presentation, MC gig, or corporate entertainment spot, I always find out: *Who is this audience? What are their challenges and pain points? What frustrates them?* This helps me understand where they are, right now, in this moment.

For corporate audiences, I write self-deprecating jokes as though I'm the annoying client or the irritating customer, and it always lands well. Meeting audiences in their frustration using humour alleviates stress, drops defences instantly, and creates an authentic connection that's delightfully fun and memorable.

Meeting Sceptics Where They Are

When I introduced magic into corporate work, it reinforced another critical lesson: meet people's scepticism before trying to lead them anywhere.

Magic is divisive. Responses range from "Amazing, I love magic!" to "That's so immature. Why would you waste your time?" I learnt you can't force magic on anyone. If someone is truly closed down, trying to lead them to amazement becomes torture for everyone.

So I started acknowledging scepticism upfront: "I know some of you might think this is silly, and that's fine. Let's just play a game and see what happens." This simple reframe transforms the dynamic.

When I acknowledge their doubts first, working *with* their preconceptions rather than *against* them, I can gently guide them somewhere unexpected. And when I meet their scepticism *and then* create a mind-blowing magical moment, the experience lands far deeper.

Meeting Crisis With Presence

Now, back to the conference and ambulance… Standing in those wings, I had a choice: perform my 10 killer jokes regardless of the room's needs, or drop my script and serve the moment.

The old me from the charity event would have marched ahead with my planned material. But I had learnt the secret: you can't lead people who don't feel met. So, I walked out slower than I normally do. Not with the high-energy sprint I normally burst onto stage with, but something true to that moment.

I looked at that room and said, "I know we're all wondering if everyone's OK. Me too. Let's take a breath together." I felt the entire room exhale their stress, like a giant balloon releasing its grip.

From that space of uncertainty and concern, I gradually guided them into warmth, connection, and, eventually, laughter. We ended up in the same place of learning and laughter that we would have landed had I started the keynote the way I usually would. We just got there in a much more cohesive, connected, and intentional way.

When I walked off stage, the event organiser looked like she had tears in her eyes. "Thank you," she said.

That experience taught me that meeting people where they are matters more than any prepared material. When people feel truly seen and genuinely met, they want to follow you. And not because they have to, but because they trust you.

Your perfect plan won't survive real-world disasters. True influence doesn't come from flawless execution. It comes from the courage to drop your script and be present to what's needed – right here, right now.

5 TRUTH BOMBS

You can't lead those you haven't met
Influence doesn't start with your agenda. It starts the moment people feel genuinely *seen*.

Name what everyone's thinking
The elephant in the room? Call it out. Acknowledging the awkward moments builds instant trust.

Meet resistance, don't bulldoze it
The moment you acknowledge resistance instead of ignoring or fighting it, it can become a powerful point of connection.

Meeting creates loyalty
Your perfect plan means nothing if people don't feel seen. Make meeting them first and understanding them a top priority.

Connection beats perfection
Real presence, with imperfections, will always win over someone who is perfectly rehearsed but disconnected.

5 QUICK WINS
(TO DO RIGHT NOW)

Read the room first
Before you say a word, pause. Scan faces. Feel the temperature. Are they energised? Exhausted? Distracted? Meet them there first.

Call out the awkward
Phone rings? Someone walks in late? Bird hits the window? Name it immediately. The room will crack up and instantly relax.

Meet before you lead
Difficult conversation ahead? Start here: "I can see you're frustrated". Acknowledge where they are, and meet any resistance *before* trying to move past it.

Do your homework
Before important meetings, research their challenges, identify their frustrations, and understand their goals. Walk in with a solid understanding of who you're connecting with.

Ask what matters
In the middle of important conversations, don't be afraid to stop and ask: "What would make this conversation truly meaningful and valuable for you right now?" Then, address that instead of just focusing on your agenda.

CHAPTER SEVEN
CONGRUENCE
The Secret Of Complete Alignment

My first joke landed beautifully.

The audience at the New York Comedy Club was warmed up, expectant, and ready for laughs. And I was living my dream; performing my first ever stand-up comedy set at one of the most legendary venues in the world.

I had very solid material about the differences I had observed between Australia and America; all fresh and all hilarious. Every word was memorised and every beat was rehearsed. And I had bullet points for each joke written on the inside of my hand as a backup… just in case.

I delivered my opening joke and got more laughs than I expected.

Then my mind went completely blank.

It wasn't a creative pause. Nor was it a strategic beat. It was a completely terrifying, 30-second freeze where I couldn't remember anything. I couldn't remember my name, let alone any joke I had ever written.

The Freeze

I stood there, like a deer in headlights. My voice suddenly went dry and hoarse and I was struggling to find words. My face and neck burned red-hot and an intense set of butterflies attacked my stomach.

The audience's faces shifted from anticipation to compassionate confusion and I could feel their empathy. They knew I had a complete blank, and they were willing me to find my way back – but that only made the stress feel heavier.

Everything felt hard, intense, suffocating.

My internal dialogue dissolved into pure terror: *Oh my gosh, oh my gosh, oh my gosh. What do I do?* My brain and my body had completely disconnected and I wasn't present at all.

I was trapped in a feedback loop of pure panic. My palms were so sweaty they looked like I'd been caught in the rain. And when I glanced down at my hand where I'd written my backup notes, it was just a giant smudge mark. The ink had run everywhere.

What am I going to do? I have four minutes left!

Everyone was staring and the lights were blinding. I looked towards the table where one of my friends was sitting: I locked eyes with her and took a big, desperate breath. In that breathing space, my material eventually came flooding back and I finished the set, which was a massive hit.

But I walked off stage gut-wrenched, feeling like I'd completely failed. All I could think about was the moment I blanked, and nothing else.

What Was Really Happening

That New York freeze wasn't an isolated incident. It was the result of a pattern that had been trapping me for years: incongruence between who I was trying to be and who I actually was in high-pressure moments – driven by a relentless need for perfectionism.

I was so dependent on delivering my scripted jokes in the early years of stand-up comedy, and so terrified of making mistakes, that I'd turned every performance into a memorisation test. I felt that if I knew every word, I was safe and protected. But scripts are prisons. They don't just create a false sense of security; they prevent real-time connection. And they're traps because if you forget even one word, everything can unravel instantly.

When you're locked into a set of predetermined steps, you can't possibly adapt to what's actually happening in the room or have true flexibility and fluidity.

For months after that New York set, my 30-second freeze replayed on loop in my mind. Unlike my Facebook disaster, where my body was overcome with obvious nerves (Chapter 4), this was different – this was my mind completely abandoning me when I needed it most.

I'd be brushing my teeth and suddenly I was back there, frozen under those lights. I'd be having coffee with friends and the memory would slam into me; that moment of complete disconnection when I needed presence most.

This was before I learnt to meet audiences where they are (Chapter 6). Instead, I was trapped in my head, trying to force others to meet me in my scripted, memorised, perfectly planned world. And when that world crumbled, I had nowhere to go.

The Trap Of Perfectionism

That incongruence didn't just show up on stage. When I published my first business-marketing book, perfectionism sabotaged me again, but this time at the finish line.

The book was engaging, well-researched, funny and informative. It was professionally proofread, copyedited, and structurally edited. As an ex-journalist, I'd even asked former colleagues from the newspaper to read it. There was no rational reason to believe there were errors. But as we know, perfectionism doesn't operate on logic.

I was so scared of a grammatical error that for six months, 700 copies sat in boxes in my apartment gathering dust.

Every time I walked past them, I felt a heavy wave of anxiety. *What if there's a typo? What if I missed something? What if readers find a mistake and think I'm unprofessional?* Every time I saw the boxes my stomach dropped.

The rational part of my brain knew this was ridiculous. But the fearful part wouldn't listen. As a result, my book's physical release date shifted from 2015 to 2016; an entire calendar year lost to phantom fears.

Those boxes became daily reminders of how perfectionism poisons our achievements. Instead of feeling proud that I'd written and completed my first book, I felt traumatised by the possibility of imperfection. My accomplishment had become a huge source of stress.

Perfectionism convinced me that the possibility of imperfection was riskier and more dangerous than doing nothing at all. And that's the trap: perfectionism poses as high standards, but it's actually fear dressed up in a very, very convincing disguise.

And it doesn't just prevent us from starting. It can sabotage us right at the moment of victory.

The Comedy Festival Transformation

In the lead-up to my first solo comedy festival show in 2013, all of my friends, and even acquaintances, threatened the same thing: "We're going to heckle you. We're going to heckle you." This was all I heard. Over and over.

I had been so focused on preparation: writing the show, testing material, marketing, design, promotion, selling tickets… I didn't once think about the fact that I would be challenged mid-show. It didn't cross my radar (which shows how green and naive I was back then).

When you're testing new material at small venues, there are very rarely hecklers. And even if there are, they're generally handled by the MC or more experienced comedians. I never entertained the idea that an actual heckler would come to my solo show.

Because I was completely out of my depth at that stage, with no experience, I was petrified. I was afraid that everything I had invested – the hours, effort, time, money, preparation – could be ruined by one determined heckler. I had no idea how to answer them or even come back to them, so I began to imagine the worst-case scenarios. My anxiety went on a loop thinking about all the ways every joke could go pear-shaped with the wrong type of provocation.

But there was no way out. As they say, the show must go on. So, I Googled "What are the most common heckle lines?" followed immediately by "What are the best comebacks?" And I printed out four pages of classic heckles and brilliant comebacks and took these with me each night on a clipboard.

I didn't hide any of this from the audience. In fact, I made it part of the show. Halfway through every performance, I stopped and announced: "This is my first comedy festival, and everyone said I'd get heckled. And I was petrified. So, this is your moment. Lights up on the audience, please. Come on, hit me with your best heckles. I promise I have a cracker response for you."

An audience member yelled out: "You suck!"

I scanned through the pages on the clipboard and replied: "And you swallow!"

The audience howled with laughter. It became an immensely funny game where the audience was challenged to come up with their best heckles, and I always had a lightning-fast comeback. As it turned out, the biggest laughs in every show came from this section.

Owning My Fear

The contrast between the New York freeze and my comedy festival show was profound.

In New York, I tried to hide my fear, memorise my way to safety, and project confidence I didn't feel. In my solo show, I completely owned my terror. I was authentic about my fear, creative with my solution, and fully aligned with my truth. My words, my energy, my intention, and my authentic experience all matched.

That alignment – that congruence – created connection, trust, and ultimately, lots of laughter. When we own our fear instead of hiding it, we become completely congruent because we're honouring every single part of who we are. This experience showed me that if we allow fear to take over, we disconnect from our creativity and new possibilities. But when we take the things that frighten us and turn them into a source of creativity, it's incredibly empowering.

How To Spot Incongruence

You've sensed it before: that moment when someone's saying all the right words but your gut is telling you something's not right. Their smile feels forced. Their laugh sounds off. Your body knows before your brain catches up.

Here are some tell-tale signs that break connection:

Disconnected Delivery

When gestures feel random or jarring, and don't connect with the actual words being spoken – like flapping your arms a lot during serious moments, or standing totally frozen while describing something exciting.

Delayed Responses

Someone might say, "Yes, I agree with you", but their head nods too late. That delay reveals the words came from their mouth, and not their conviction.

Physical Betrayal

When words claim confidence but their body tells the opposite story; shoulders hunched, arms crossed defensively, or fidgeting nervously. This body language screams, "Get me out of here!" louder than any verbal message.

Emotional Mismatch

Saying "I'm so excited!" with a flat, lifeless expression. Or sharing a deeply personal, powerful story while expressing it with the same monotone delivery you would use to read a shopping list.

Speaking From Memory Without Meaning

Reciting words like a script rather than expressing genuine truth. This happens when there's no real connection to what's being said.

When there's no authentic connection to a message, we disconnect. It's as simple as that.

Building Congruence

After owning my fear and experiencing how powerful this was, I realised there were specific things that helped me achieve that alignment – lessons I now apply every time I step on stage or into a workshop:

Know your intention before you speak. At my comedy show, my intention was crystal clear: *I'm terrified of hecklers, but I'm going to face this fear and make it part of the experience.* When I stayed anchored to that truth, instead of pretending not to feel afraid, everything aligned.

Find the part that feels real to you. Even in my fear, I could connect emotionally to the creativity of my solution. When you connect to what's authentic, your body comes alive naturally, just like mine did when I pulled out that clipboard.

Ground yourself in your truth. Before high-pressure moments, I say to myself, "You can do this". I trust and listen to my inner truth instead of the voice of fear.

Let your emotion guide your delivery when it comes from a place of honesty. When I confessed to the audience that I was petrified, my voice carried that weight. When I revealed my creative solution, my excitement was genuine. I stopped *performing* emotions and started truly feeling and tuning into them.

Own every part of yourself. The biggest lesson from my debut comedy festival season was: **Embrace what scares you most, instead of hiding from it.**

When Congruence Clicks

In my public speaking workshops, I witness the moment congruence kicks in, and it's one of the most beautiful transformations to see.

A student will be hunched over, about to present while their entire body screams, "Where's the closest exit?" Their voice is shaky, their posture is contracted, and their energy is scattered. Every part of them is telling a different story.

But then we work on alignment. We cover breathing techniques, how to stand in an expansive position so their physical presence matches their message, and other fast, fun, and effective tools for instant change. The moment they stop fighting themselves and start understanding how to work with their bodies, congruence kicks in immediately.

Their voice drops and becomes steady. They get a sparkle in their eyes. Their shoulders open. They're anchored in their power. And their presence fills the room. Teaching someone how to discover, or regain, their confidence naturally leads to complete alignment between who they are and how they show up. And it's one of the greatest gifts I can give.

What blows my mind is that there's an expectation that just because we communicate every single day, we should know how to present in a meeting or speak at the front of a boardroom. The skills are different. The pressure's different. Our body goes through different physiological, mental, and emotional responses when we have stress hormones flooding through our system.

And if we don't know how to use our body confidently – even if we have the most amazing message in the world – our delivery is likely to be too fast, too boring, too monotone, or too flat. People will immediately switch off.

Why Alignment Changes Everything

Now, every time I step on stage – whether for keynotes, MC-ing, magic, mentalism, or corporate comedy – I'm completely different from that terrified performer who froze in New York.

I don't memorise scripts or jokes. My PowerPoint slides only feature images, which gives me structure without traps, and flexibility without chaos. And for comedy, I take a simple set list.

When nerves show up (and they still do), I don't fight them or hide them. I acknowledge them. I welcome them and I breathe through them using the 4-2-4 technique I learnt through a body-movement modality called Feldenkrais. Breathe in for four seconds, hold for two seconds, and then breathe out for four seconds. This is a powerful technique because when we focus on numbers, we can't also be trapped in anxious thoughts. Plus, it gives our brain the experience of taking control of our physiology in challenging moments, which gives us proof that we can regulate ourselves, even when fear tries to ambush us.

Most importantly, I ground myself in my truth before every presentation. I connect to my genuine intention, my authentic message, and my real reason for being there.

The reality is, I still have fears, and fear shows up in countless ways. But I know that the fears I choose to face and deconstruct always become my greatest strengths and the defining moments in life. Our fears don't have to limit us.

When every part of you is telling the same story, that's when the magic happens. When your words, your tonality, your expression, your energy, your intention, and your truth all align, people don't just hear your message, they feel it.

Congruence is the glue that holds influence together when the stakes are high, and, in fact, especially when they're high. And when someone tries to throw you off centre, your congruence is what keeps you standing in your power. Because when you own your story – all of it, even the scary parts – you always win.

5 TRUTH BOMBS

Own your fear, don't hide it
When you stop pretending to be fearless and authentically own what scares you, it doesn't make you weak. It makes you bulletproof.

Perfectionism is a creativity and productivity killer
The pursuit of flawless execution doesn't protect you. It paralyses you and blocks every risk worth taking.

Your energy screams louder than your words
People sense incongruence instantly, even when you're saying all the right things.

Congruence is magnetic
When every part of your expression and delivery is aligned, people don't decide to believe you; they just do.

Authenticity is your unfair advantage
Being authentically you creates more impact than any 'perfectly polished' performance ever could.

5 QUICK WINS
(TO DO RIGHT NOW)

Know your why
Before any conversation, ask: "What do I genuinely want to achieve here?" Answer honestly.

Congruence check
Quick scan: Does your posture and energy match the intention of your words?

Spot your own BS
Identify one thing you're saying that you don't fully believe. You know what it is. Either change your words or change your belief.

4-2-4 instant calm
Breathe through your nerves. Breathe in for four seconds, hold for two seconds, and then exhale for four seconds. Do this three times in a row and feel the immediate calm it brings. This breathing technique instantly centres you into the present moment. (Play around with the timing to find what works best for your body.)

Your alignment test
Ask yourself: "Are my words, tonality, expression, energy, and intention all pointing in the same direction *right now*?" Awareness is the first step towards creating change.

CHAPTER EIGHT
EMBODY

The Secret Power Of Being Unapologetically Human

I was wearing a fake silver bling necklace with a "J" for Lil Jords (my rapper name), zebra print leggings, heavy sunglasses, and doing my absolute worst rap dance moves in front of a camera.

This was my hip-hop alter ego, my "creative bombshell" that was going to launch me to YouTube stardom in 2011. I'd created a YouTube channel, Twitter account, Facebook page, and bought the liljords.com domain so nobody else could grab it. I spent days writing satirical rap songs about Justin Bieber, Kim Kardashian, Lady Gaga and other pop stars. I headed to an audio producer's studio to record vocals and lay tracks, and then spent hours editing the videos.

I had different costumes for each celebrity I rapped about. For Paris Hilton, I got a tiny handbag with a plastic chihuahua inside. For Lady Gaga, I wore a blonde wig. For Justin Bieber, I sported a purple shirt. The zebra print leggings were for Kim Kardashian. Every single video featured me in those heavy sunglasses and ridiculous bling necklace, doing dance moves that would make anyone with real rhythm physically cringe.

I invested just as much effort into Lil Jords as I did into all the successful online music content at my radio station job. The radio content absolutely popped on social media. But Lil Jords? Nine rap videos, 600 total views, and only 25 Facebook followers… all family and friends.

The Devastating Reality

It was distressing to watch those view counts stay so low. The worst part? People in my life told me it was "really good", and then, years later, admitted it was the worst thing they'd ever seen. They just didn't want to crush my spirit.

I'd spent money on costumes, backdrops, and editing software. I spent hours researching synonyms for my "dope" new attitude. I tweeted my videos directly to the stars I rapped about: Rihanna, Paris Hilton, even Perez Hilton… Naturally, nobody ever responded.

When I watch those clips now, I can barely look. The costumes are horrendous, and I can categorically declare I am not a rapper and I had no captive audience. Clearly no one was interested in a girl like me attempting hardcore satirical rap. (Or perhaps my comedy genius was just too advanced for that era. I'll never know.)

The Exhaustion Of Self-Editing

Looking back, the Lil Jords disaster wasn't random at all. It was part of a bigger pattern: trying to force myself into trending boxes instead of finding my authentic voice. But underneath my creative attempts was a deeper struggle – I was performing what I thought people wanted. And it was the result of spending years being too afraid to show the full spectrum of who I really was.

From Hiding To Healing

One... two... three... four... five... six... seven. That's how many times I checked every light switch when I left my apartment. Seven laps around my place because I was convinced that if I didn't check them all, in sequence, something terrible would happen.

I had obsessive tendencies (never diagnosed but definitely present) that significantly impacted several aspects of my life. Not all areas, but enough to be exhausting. I'd flee parties mid-conversation, convinced I'd left the iron on despite not using it for six weeks. Logic didn't stand a chance against my anxiety. I was also a hypochondriac.

So self-deprecating humour became my armour. *Oh, you think I'm weird? Let me beat you to the punchline.* I thought if I could laugh at myself first, it would hurt less when others inevitably did.

But underneath that laughter was always a quiet sting: *Why am I like this? What's wrong with me? Why can't I just be normal?*

So, when it came to creating my first solo show for the comedy festival in 2013, I did what any neurotic creative would do: I gave it a medical theme. The show was called "Social Needia: The Epidemic". It was about my addiction to social media, a three-day enforced detox I took, and the lessons I learnt along the way. And because of the medical theme, I made a decision that terrified me: I was going to put my shame in the spotlight.

I wrote jokes about my obsessive behaviours, my hypochondria, my anxieties, and my fears. It was risky to expose myself like this. The only fallback was: *Well, they don't know it's all true. I could be making it up.*

I had at least 12 jokes about the parts of me I'd been trying to hide, fix, or scrub away for years. The checking rituals. The intrusive thoughts. The anxiety loops. And they weren't throwaway lines; they were deeply personal. I was literally putting my shame in the spotlight and hoping people would laugh with me... instead of at me.

The first night, standing backstage, I was convinced I'd made a terrible mistake. *What are they going to think? What if this confirms everything I've feared about myself? What if my biggest fan turns out to be my therapist taking notes?*

But then something magical happened.

When I delivered these jokes, they were an absolute hit. That vulnerability, that rawness, that absolute truth... People loved it, admired it, respected it, and connected with it.

Writing those jokes was therapy, and performing them proved even more healing. That's because when you name your shame and hold it up to the light, it starts to lose its power over you. As Brené Brown explains, vulnerability isn't weakness; it's the origin of creativity, innovation, and change.[13]

There's a self-awareness tool called the Johari Window, created by Joseph Luft and Harrington Ingham in 1955, that perfectly explains what comedy did for me.[14] It maps how we show up in the world through four quadrants:

Open Area / Arena – what everyone knows about you

Blind Spot – what others see but you don't

Hidden Area / Facade – what you know but keep private

Unknown Area – what nobody knows about you, not even you

Here's where comedy became transformational. It allowed me to take everything I would normally bury in that Hidden Area – my fears, my flaws, my perceived failures, and everything I was embarrassed about – and bring it all into the light. So, for the first time ever, instead of feeling shame, I used these aspects of myself to create connection. Instead of feeling judgement, I created moments of both laughter and healing.

And after that comedy festival run, magically, unexpectedly, and to my complete surprise, I stopped doing laps. I stopped checking light switches. The rituals that had controlled aspects of my life for the previous few years simply… stopped.

But the real miracle wasn't just in my behaviour; it was emotional. For years, I'd carried the weight of thinking something was fundamentally wrong with me. Humour healed my relationship with myself. I learnt comedy isn't just entertainment – it became my most powerful healing tool.

Permission To Be Real

On night seven of that festival run, a woman in her 50s approached me at the bar. "I have to tell you something," she said, tears in her eyes. "I've been checking my stove for 20 years. Every night before bed. Sometimes twice. I have never told anyone." Then she smiled. "Thank you."

That's when it hit me: vulnerability wasn't just healing for me – it was permission for others to heal too. After every show, people would share their version: "I do that too!", "That's totally my husband!", and "I thought I was the only one!" My shame had become their permission to stop hiding.

Our flaws aren't flaws. They're what make us human. And our honesty about them creates deep and profound connections. But that was just the beginning of understanding what authentic influence could do.

Looking back, the contrast was so clear: Lil Jords had been about performing what I thought would go viral; while comedy was about expressing my authentic voice. Instead of hiding behind costumes and personas, I was using my real experiences – my neuroses, my struggles, my genuine perspective – as the foundation for connection. I wasn't just being authentic. I was taking my authenticity and amplifying it to create comedy that came from a real, true, and emotionally charged place.

The Real Secret

In those moments of vulnerability, with nothing but a microphone, a spotlight, and a ridiculous amount of anxiety, I learnt the most important lesson about influence (which I mention in Chapter 1):

The best kind doesn't come from polish. It always comes from presence. There's no hiding when you're on stage, no pretending when your punchline bombs, and no faking it when your entire job is to say, "Here I am – please laugh with me". The skills that make you a great comedian are exactly the same ones that make you an influential leader:

Authenticity – You can't perform your way to connection.

Vulnerability – People don't trust perfect; they trust real.

Reframing – The ability to find a different angle and help people see a problem or challenge in a brand new light.

Resilience – Your ability to bounce back isn't built in air-conditioned boardrooms. It's created in moments when everything goes wrong and you keep going anyway.

Comedy didn't just heal me. It gave me the most unshakeable foundation for everything I do now – as a speaker, MC, performer, mentalist, and human being.

The Perfection Epidemic

We're living in an era of imitation, where countless people are mimicking the same personalities online, hoping to hack success. The paradox? The word 'authenticity' is used more than ever; yet so many messages and voices sound alike.

And the pressure to be perfect doesn't stop at social media. Through hundreds of workshops I've run, from metropolitan hubs to country towns, I see the same struggle: people wrestle with the pressure to be "the expert" – believing that if they don't know everything about a topic, they've failed. They'd rather stay silent than risk being wrong. The truth is, if someone stands up these days and claims to have all the answers, run a mile. It's impossible. Even AI models with endless data points don't know everything. When humans pretend they do, that's not expertise – it's insecurity masked as certainty.

I learnt this lesson the hard way at a keynote presentation many years ago. My topic was communicating across generations, specifically how older generations could maximise the strengths of their millennial employees.

During the Q&A at the end, someone raised their hand: "I'm a millennial, managing up. I'm managing a baby boomer. What do I do?"

What I should have said was: "Great question, but that's not my zone of genius, nor is it my area of expertise. I'll do some research and come back to you." But I felt like I needed to answer. One of my agents was watching me for the first time and *I* felt I needed to be "the expert". So I started answering. You know that sinking feeling when you're speaking and you know what you're saying is wrong, but you're too committed to stop? That's exactly what happened and it's embarrassing. You can feel it and the audience can feel it too.

That experience taught me to never pretend to have answers when I don't. If I don't know something or I have made a mistake, I embody it. I own it in all its glory. The courage to say "I don't know" builds more trust than fumbling through fake expertise. And it empowers you with a deep sense of freedom.

Once you own what's real – the mistakes, gaps and mess – doing anything else feels impossible. You also start noticing how carefully others hide behind polish. I watch this in my workshops constantly: students struggling to share their truth, own their strengths, or say "I'm the right person to deliver this message", especially when that message comes from their messiest moments.

We live in a culture that insists we don't shine too brightly, that talking about wins makes us arrogant, and that sharing accomplishments means we're showing off. As a result, people stay small. They're too afraid to own what truly makes them extraordinary.

We spend too much time worrying about others' opinions, and in the process we disconnect from our true essence. If we instead spent all that energy focused on giving ourselves permission to be who we truly are, it would radically change our presence, and the impact we have on everyone around us.

Fully You, Fully Powerful

So drop the performance and show up exactly as you are. Are you an artist? Own it. A secret poet? Brilliant. A recovering perfectionist?

Raises hand

Whatever makes you different – that is your magic.

The moment I embraced my own differences, I began to recognise the beauty in everyone else's. This allows me to instantly see other people's quirks and unique experiences as powerful strengths – and certainly nothing they should be afraid of, and nothing they should try to hide. Every single thing we've done until this point has made us who we are, and all of that should be embraced, celebrated, and appreciated.

In this age of digital overwhelm, we don't need more polished personas performing picture-perfect and heavily filtered versions of themselves. We need more people willing to show up as they truly are – quirks, flaws, brilliance, and all. Because when you stop hiding, you create ripple effects you never expected.

And when you own your story, including the messy, imperfect, unfiltered, and beautifully human parts, you give others permission to own theirs too. And the permission to stop hiding.

I'm not saying you need to share your therapy sessions in board meetings. I'm saying that when you stop concealing the human parts of yourself – your mistakes, your moments of growth, your struggles, your big 'aha moments', and your real personality – you become someone people actually want to listen to.

When you stop trying to be impressive and start being real, you become unforgettable.

5 TRUTH BOMBS

Your weirdness is your magic
The quirks you've spent years hiding? Those are exactly what make you unforgettable.

Authenticity over performance... every time
Real always beats perfect. People can smell fake from a mile away, and they'll choose the truth every time.

Your vulnerability is a permission slip for others
The moment you own your story without apology, you give others permission to also drop their masks.

Your differences are your greatest strengths
In a world of highly curated content, being unapologetically you is the most radical thing you can do.

Embodiment creates transformation
When you show up as your full, unfiltered self, you don't just influence people, you inspire them.

5 QUICK WINS
(TO DO RIGHT NOW)

Drop the mask
Pick one area where you're performing a curated version of yourself instead of being real. And choose to stop performing… Starting now.

Own your failure
Tell someone about a time you massively messed up and what it taught you. Claim the lesson out loud.

The power of "I don't know"
If you don't have the answer, say so, instead of fumbling through fake expertise.

Get personal
In your next conversation, drop one genuinely human detail about yourself: something real… and notice how fast people lean in.

Take one new creative step
Have you always wanted to paint? To sing? To learn a new language? To write a book? Start today. Your differences are your magic. Act on your passions.

THE PERMISSION YOU'VE BEEN WAITING FOR

As I finish writing this, I'm thinking about that girl doing seven laps around her apartment, obsessively checking light switches. About the comedian who bombed so spectacularly on a cruise ship that passengers told her to get off in the middle of the ocean. About the woman who dressed as a giant Facebook Like and got escorted out of Facebook's headquarters because her body language screamed guilt when she was telling the truth.

If I could jump into a time machine, I would tell her: Your weirdness isn't something to fix, your failures aren't something to hide, and your humanness isn't something to apologise for. They're your superpowers. And they will become your greatest assets in comedy, speaking, MC work, magic, mentalism… and, of course, ultimately, in learning about influence.

The Cost Of Staying Hidden

Your journey won't look like mine. But I imagine you'll have your own moments of hiding, your own masks you've perfected, and your own fears of being "too much" or "not enough".

When you keep *performing* instead of *connecting*, it's exhausting. You walk into every room calculating what version of yourself to show. You second-guess every word, and you leave interactions wondering if they liked *you* or just the character you played. And the worst part? You watch others get amazing opportunities because they're willing to show up as themselves. The world doesn't need another perfect performance. It needs your perfectly *imperfect* truth.

What Becomes Possible

You now have the complete PRESENCE framework:

Perceive
Truly see and listen with your whole body.

Reimagine
Envision new possibilities and bring them to life through unwavering belief.

Empower
Believe in others so deeply that they begin to believe in themselves.

Signals
Master non-verbal cues that speak louder than words.

Expression
Use language that opens minds and creates possibilities.

Navigate

Meet people where they are, then guide them forward.

Congruence

Complete alignment between what you think, feel, say, and do.

Embody

Bring your whole, imperfect, magnificent self to every interaction.

The Challenge

But frameworks mean nothing without action.

So start now: In your next conversation, try one tool from this book. Practise Glitter Chest instead of scrolling on your phone as you walk into a meeting. Use the meet-then-lead principle in a difficult conversation. Replace "but" with "and" and notice what shifts. Own your fear instead of hiding it. Make meaningful eye contact. Share your actual opinion instead of what you think people want to hear. Own your expertise without apologising. And be the person who walks into rooms and changes the energy. Not because you've perfected every technique, but because you've stopped performing and started connecting.

And watch what happens. When you show up authentically, you give others permission to do the same. Your authenticity creates space for their truth. Your vulnerability invites their courage. And your willingness to be human helps them drop their masks too.

The path to authentic influence is different for everyone, but the destination is the same: the courage to be fully yourself. This creates the foundation for true connection.

When you embody PRESENCE, you don't just change your life path – you give everyone around you permission to be more human, more creative, and more connected. And you inspire others. That's the real power of PRESENCE. It's contagious. And when you embrace it, you become a catalyst for transformation.

So I challenge you to be the fullest, boldest, and most unapologetically human version of yourself.

Own it all: your awesomeness, your awkwardness, your mistakes, and all of your magic.

The world is ready for the real you.

LET'S CONNECT

Curious? Inspired? Have a question about the book, or something to share? Drop me a line. I'd love to hear from you!

My email: jordana@jordanab.me

Visit my website: https://jordanab.com.au

@jordanaborensztajn

#jordanaborensztajn

@iamjordanaborensztajn

jordanab.com.au

... AND JOIN THE JOURNEY

Keep your momentum going with weekly tools, tips, and challenges from the PRESENCE framework.

Sign up to my newsletter to get the magic delivered straight to your inbox.

Sign up here: https://littlebooks.biz

Or scan the QR code below:

littlebooks.biz

ABOUT THE AUTHOR

Jordana Borensztajn brings high energy, deep insights, and infectious laughter to stages worldwide.

She has written four books and performed two sold-out shows at the Melbourne International Comedy Festival. Her extraordinary career path – from comedy clubs to corporate stages across three continents – gives her a rare and entertaining perspective on the art of human connection.

Before stepping into the world of comedy and speaking, Jordana worked as a journalist with News Corp Australia and as National Online Music Editor at Nova Entertainment.

She fuses her strong media foundation with powerful stagecraft to bring a unique blend of storytelling, humour, and insight to every audience she meets.

Today, Jordana is a keynote speaker, TEDx presenter, event MC, corporate humourist, public speaking trainer, and communications expert. She electrifies crowds with her signature mix of magic, mentalism, comedy, and razor-sharp insights, and she masterfully blends entertainment with education, transforming every keynote, workshop, and event, into an unforgettable experience.

Whether inspiring hundreds from the main stage or guiding small groups in intimate workshops, Jordana specialises in creating powerful 'aha moments' that lead to true and lasting change.

Her mission is refreshingly simple: educate through joy, inspire through laughter, and empower people to step boldly into who they are meant to become.

ENDNOTES

1. University of Texas Permian Basin. (n.d.). How Much of Communication Is Nonverbal? *UTPB Online*. https://online.utpb.edu/about-us/articles/communication/how-much-of-communication-is-nonverbal.
2. Becker, J. (2023, March 31). *Shaping Sara Blakely: Meet the Billionaire Founder of Spanx*. SUCCESS. https://www.success.com/shaping-sara-blakely-meet-the-billionaire-founder-of-spanx/
3. Ranganathan, V. K., Siemionow, V., Liu, J. Z., Sahgal, V., & Yue, G. H. (2004). From mental power to muscle power – gaining strength by using the mind. *Neuropsychologia*, 42(7), 944–956. https://www.docdroid.net/Bv2DHXf/101016-at-jneuropsychologia200311018-pdf.
4. Rosenthal, R., & Jacobson, L. (1968). *Pygmalion in the classroom: Teacher expectation and pupils' intellectual development*. New York: Holt, Rinehart & Winston. [Note: Though the original study has faced criticism for methodological issues and limited replication, the general concept of expectation effects remains valid. It is known as the Pygmalion Effect]
5. Cosmides, L. and Tooby, J. (1997). *Evolutionary Psychology: A Primer*. Center for Evolutionary Psychology, University of California, Santa Barbara. http://cogweb.ucla.edu/ep/EP-primer.html.
6. Goldstein, S. (2025). Why We're Wired to Read Emotions in Expressions, Not Sounds. *Psychology Today*. https://www.psychologytoday.com/us/blog/common-sense-science/202507/why-were-wired-to-read-emotions-in-expressions-not-sounds.
7. Paul Ekman Group. (2018). *Micro Expressions Training | Subtle Expression Training*. https://www.paulekman.com/micro-expressions-training-tools.
8. Willis, J., & Todorov, A. (2006). First impressions: Making up your mind after a 100-ms exposure to a face. *Psychological Science*, 17(7), 592-598. https://journals.sagepub.com/doi/10.1111/j.1467-9280.2006.01750.x.
9. Joy, R. (2019). Smiling with Your Eyes: What Exactly Is a Duchenne Smile? *Healthline*. https://www.healthline.com/health/duchenne-smile#muscles-used.
10. Stanborough, R.J. (2019). What Is a Duchenne Smile and How Can It Influence Other People? *Healthline*. https://www.healthline.com/health/duchenne-smile.
11. Van Edwards, V. (2025, January 26). 60 Hand gestures you should be using and their meaning. *Science of People*. https://www.scienceofpeople.com/hand-gestures.
12. Binetti, N., Harrison, C., Coutrot, A., Johnston, A., & Mareschal, I. (2016). Pupil dilation as an index of preferred mutual gaze duration. *Royal Society Open Science*, 3(7), 160086. https://doi.org/10.1098/rsos.160086.
13. Brown, B. (2012, March). Listening to shame [Video]. TED. https://www.ted.com/talks/brene_brown_listening_to_shame.
14. The Decision Lab. (2021). *Johari Window*. The Decision Lab. https://thedecisionlab.com/reference-guide/psychology/johari-window

LONGUEVILLE
MEDIA

Produced 2025 by
Longueville Media
PO Box 205
Haberfield NSW 2045 Australia
www.longmedia.com.au

Text copyright © 2025 Jordana Borensztajn

All rights reserved. No part of this publication may be reproduced or transmitted in any form or by any means, electronic or mechanical, including photocopying, recording or by any information storage and retrieval system, without the prior permission in writing from the author and copyright holder.

The information provided in the book is presented solely for educational and entertainment purposes on the subjects discussed. It is the intent of the author to provide information of a general nature. The author is not a registered psychologist or professional counsellor, financial planner, adviser, accountant, medical practitioner or legal advisor. The information in this book is not intended to be taken as (or be in substitution for obtaining) independent professional medical, legal, tax, business, financial, marketing or any other type of advice. In the event that you use, misuse or rely on any of the information in this book, the author assumes no responsibility or liability for your actions and its consequences including without limitation, any loss, claim, damages, costs or expenses.
The author makes no warranties or representations about the accuracy of the information or the suitability of the information for your personal circumstances.
The stories in this book are based on the author's recollections of past events.

For the National Library of Australia Cataloguing-in-Publication entry visit
www.nla.gov.au

ISBN Paperback: 978-1-7640030-2-5
ISBN Print on Demand: 978-1-7640030-4-9

Structural editing and copyediting: David Longfield and Siobhan Gallagher
Developmental editing: Claude.ai
Cover art: Yulia Glam/Shutterstock.com

www.ingramcontent.com/pod-product-compliance
Lightning Source LLC
Chambersburg PA
CBHW061728070526
44583CB00024B/3054